MY IDEAL BOOKSHELF

MY IDEAL BOOKSHELF

Art by Jane Mount | *Edited by* Thessaly La Force

LITTLE, BROWN AND COMPANY

NEW YORK | BOSTON | LONDON

Little, Brown and Company
Hachette Book Group
237 Park Avenue, New York, NY 10017
littlebrown.com

First Edition: November 2012

Little, Brown and Company is a division of Hachette Book Group, Inc., and is celebrating its 175th anniversary in 2012. The Little, Brown name and logo are trademarks of Hachette Book Group, Inc.

The publisher is not responsible for websites (or their content) that are not owned by the publisher.

The Hachette Speakers Bureau provides a wide range of authors for speaking events. To find out more, go to hachettespeakersbureau.com or call (866) 376-6591.

Text on page 169 by Patti Smith. © 2010 by Patti Smith. By permission of HarperCollins Publishers.

The illustration on the cover of this book represents the covers of beloved books that were selected by contributors to *My Ideal Bookshelf* as being among their favorites. The illustration is not intended as a literal representation of the books.

Source editions for cover art, from left to right:
Sea of Poppies, by Amitav Ghosh, Viking Canada; *Mystery Train: Images of America in Rock 'n' Roll Music,* 5th ed., by Greil Marcus, Plume; *The Catcher in the Rye,* by J. D. Salinger, Little, Brown and Company; *Pride and Prejudice,* by Jane Austen, Penguin Classics; *Alexander Girard Designs for Herman Miller,* by Leslie A. Piña, Schiffer Publishing; *The Power Broker: Robert Moses and the Fall of New York,* by Robert A. Caro, Vintage; *The Little Prince,* by Antoine de Saint-Exupéry, Harcourt Children's Books

Library of Congress Cataloging-in-Publication Data

My ideal bookshelf / art by Jane Mount ; edited by Thessaly La Force.—First edition.
    pages cm
  ISBN 978-0-316-20090-5
  1. Books and reading—Psychological aspects.   2. Books and reading—United States.   3. Books in art.   I. Mount, Jane, illustrator.   II. La Force, Thessaly, editor of compilation.
  Z1003.M985 2012
  028'.9—dc23   2012020016

10 9 8 7 6 5 4 3 2

Book design by Fearn Cutler de Vicq

WOR

Printed in United States of America

To our parents,
who read to us when we were little,
and who treated the public library like day care.

———◆•◀▶•◆———

—•· Contents ·•—

The Contributors

— ❧ Preface ❧ —

The assignment sounds straightforward enough. Select a small shelf of books that represent *you*— the books that have changed your life, that have made you who you are today, your favorite favorites. You begin, perhaps, by walking over to your bookshelf and skimming the spines on the top shelf. You pull down a handful that you remember loving; you grab a couple that you read over and over again. Some you know just by the color of their dust jackets. One is in tatters—it was passed down by your mother—and it's dog-eared and carefully held together by tape and tenderness. The closer you look, the trickier the task turns out to be.

Maybe there's that one book you no longer own because you gave it away to a dear friend. And then, too, what you select today may be completely different from what you would assemble tomorrow—but that's the beauty of the exercise. It's a snapshot of you in a moment of time. You could build an ideal bookshelf every year of your life, and it would be completely different. And just as satisfying.

We asked more than one hundred creative people in a variety of disciplines from around the world to do exactly this. Chefs and architects, writers and fashion designers, filmmakers and ballet dancers all agreed to share their ideal bookshelves. It's an eclectic bunch, to be sure. Some of the contributors are our friends and acquaintances; others are people we have admired from afar. There's no organizing principle behind whom we've chosen or why—except that if this book were to symbolize *our* ideal bookshelf, then everyone in here would have a place on it. We like to imagine that if we threw a big party and invited everyone in *My Ideal Bookshelf,* all of us would have a terrific time.

For ease of browsing, we have arranged this book alphabetically by contributor, the way a traditional bookshelf might be arranged by the authors' last names. The beauty of this seemingly ordered approach is the happenstance juxtapositions that result: Stefan Sagmeister, for instance, sits between Alex Ross and George Saunders, while John Jeremiah Sullivan appears on the page after his longtime editor Lorin Stein. You'll also see that some of the shelves are in dialogue with one another even across larger leaps of pages, as when Atul Gawande places Malcolm Gladwell's book on his shelf or Chuck Klosterman selects a work by Jonathan Lethem for his. These are conversations between books and readers that would be hard to envision taking place anywhere else. The short bit of text that accompanies each painting was drawn from interviews we conducted with each of the contributors.

There's a lot we've learned in the process of creating this book. That we're woefully underread is a given. It's no great surprise that Haruki Murakami and David Foster Wallace are popular authors, or that Wallace Stevens is a favorite poet. Or that *Lolita* and *One Hundred Years of Solitude* are novels beloved by many. But who would have guessed that Lydia Davis would appear on more shelves than George Eliot? Or that Walker Percy's *The Moviegoer* would be more popular than John Updike's *Rabbit Run*?

There are hidden gems in this collection—you will find books you never knew existed. You might be shamed into finally picking up *Ulysses* or Proust. You will discover kindred readers—others who, like you, see the common thread between Olafur Eliasson and Elizabeth David, between Maxine Hong Kingston and John Keats.

Certain shelves, once painted, are illuminating in unforeseeable ways. Jorie Graham's books are, fittingly, the colors of the grass and the sea. The titles in Simon Doonan's shelf pop in the most delightful fashion. Tony Hawk's selection vibrates with a punkish, electric energy. And Junot Díaz's possesses a ferocity and warmth that are mirrored in his writing.

The writers we asked to participate often began by listing titles first, whereas the designers and illustrators also considered what colors and shapes on the spine would be interesting to paint. Some contributors have bookshelves that match their personalities. Take James Franco, whose books literally overflow on the page, not unlike his own limitless capacity for conceiving new projects. Or Pico Iyer, whose trim selection conforms to his ascetic life in rural Japan. There are unusual bookends and objects in these paintings that remind us of what kinds of things we like to keep close to the books we love—such as the tea set and stuffed creatures belonging to Francine Prose's granddaughter, which sit next to Francine's volumes of Chekhov.

While the voyeuristic element cannot be denied—each time a contributor gave us a final selection of books, we felt almost as if we were peering into his or her bathroom cabinet—we hope that these shelves will also inspire. Not because they outline a path to creative success—after all, reading the books that Jennifer Egan or Lawrence Lessig have chosen won't turn you into either one of them—but because reading is how so many of us began creatively. And it's what so many of us return to.

We made this book because we love to read. And perhaps we're guilty of sentimentalizing the book as an object. But in an era when digital technology (of which we are nevertheless fans) threatens irreversibly to change our reading experience, there is nothing that parallels the physical book. There is nothing like its weight and smell and the crackle of its spine.

Daniel Handler once said of Maira Kalman that she "wanted to paint small objects, ordinary objects that could only become magical when an artist was painting them or when someone was looking at them and remembering something magical." That's exactly how we feel about painting the spines of all the books in *My Ideal Bookshelf*. The spine is a part of the book that is often overlooked and that is totally lost in the digital age; letting them stand brightly together on the page, rendered with the human strokes of a painter's brush, makes them that much more special.

We hope that at the end of this—after you've thumbed through these pages and examined the bookshelves of everyone in here and looked at the index in the back—you'll begin to think about what it might mean to create your own ideal bookshelf. What are the books that have made you who you are?

So much depends on where you, the reader, are—physically and metaphorically—when you decide to pick up a book and give it a chance. Which explains why there's no such thing as one ideal bookshelf; there is no ur-bookshelf. It would be a mistake to try to read this book with that goal in mind. In the end, the one element that links all the ideal bookshelves in these pages is the never-ending search. We're all still hunting, still hoping to discover one more book that we'll love and treasure for the rest of our lives.

The more that you read,

the more things you will know.

The more that you learn,

the more places you'll go.

—DR. SEUSS

MY IDEAL BOOKSHELF

Hugh Acheson

chef + cookbook author

There is this distorted explanation of Southern food—that it's fatty and overcooked and lard-infused and so on. And it's not really true. It's a certain flash of Southern cooking that's been run through the mud so many times that people think that's all we eat. But there's a lot more to it.

Take something as simple as pickles: pickling and canning are so ubiquitous to the South, people have been doing them both for two hundred years and documenting the processes. So you can go back and find recipes for pickled nasturtium seeds, which someone used to replace capers in a traditional Southern dish. It's endless, the depth of Southern cooking.

> *If you immerse yourself in food, you start to understand the other aspects of flavors and profiles and nuances that can't be written down.*

Some of these books are inspirations for me, like *New Southern Cooking* by Nathalie Dupree and *The Taste of Country Cooking* by Edna Lewis. Edna passed away about six years ago, but she was a grande dame of Southern food and Southern food writing. Here was a black woman in the 1960s—her grandmother was an emancipated slave—cooking in New York and the South. Not as a cook, but as a chef. And she writes from this perspective that's so agrarian, deep-rooted, and knowledgeable but also so natural. I admire her relationship with food.

That's a first-edition Chez Panisse book that I bought in Ottawa, Canada, probably in the late eighties or early nineties. It is so beautifully written, and I love what Alice has done, but Paul Bertolli is the real force behind that book. It's so wonderfully vague. His recipe for risotto talks about how you just know when it's done. And it's true! If you immerse yourself in food, you start to understand the other aspects of flavors and profiles and nuances that can't be written down. It's how it smells when it's done. Or you know how if something is oversalted, if it's gleaming in that way that means it's pulling out too much moisture? He's really good at getting that across.

I was on *Top Chef.* I don't regret doing it. This is the industry that I'm in. It's always cool to me that somebody has decided to make a competitive cooking show around it. It's interesting to see the dynamic of kitchens; they are high-fueled places, pent-up environments, and it's a pretty addictive thing to watch. Cooking is known as one of the most stressful careers of all, and it is.

Aller

CIDER BEANS, WILD GREENS, AND DANDELION JELLY

10

Southern Belly John T. Edge THE ULTIMATE Food Lover's Companion to the South

Terrines, Pâtés & Galantines THE GOOD COOK/TECHNIQUES & RECIPES

Foods of the World

Classic French Cooking

SLATER

Tender

SPEGO PRESS

Dornenburg and Page

Culinary Artistry

Wiley

LAROUSSE Gastronomique

Crown

CHEZ PANISSE COOKING

Paul Bertolli with Alice Waters

RANDOM HOUSE

JAMES BEARD'S AMERICAN COOKERY

LITTLE, BROWN

INGREDIENTS & RECIPES

LEON

ALLEGRA McEVEDY

NATHALIE DUPREE NEW SOUTHERN COOKING

Georgia

THE TASTE OF COUNTRY COOKING

EDNA LEWIS

KNOPF

Chimamanda Ngozi Adichie
◄• writer •►

I grew up in a university town in Nigeria. I was an early reader, and what I read, as a young child, was mostly British and American books. I was also an early writer. And when I began to write, at about the age of seven—stories in pencil with crayon illustrations, which my poor mother was obligated to read—I wrote exactly the kinds of stories I was reading.

All my characters were white and drank ginger beer, because the British characters in the books I read drank a lot of ginger beer. Never mind that I had no idea what ginger beer was. My characters ate apples and played in the snow and talked about the weather, how lovely it was that the sun had come out. This despite the fact that I had never been outside Nigeria; I lived in a world where the people were mostly black and ate mangoes and didn't have snow and never talked about the weather because there was no need to. I loved those books. They stirred my imagination and opened up new worlds for me, but the unintended consequence was that I did not consciously, actively, know that people like me—little girls with skin

I did not consciously, actively, know that people like me—little girls with skin the color of chocolate, whose kinky hair did not form ponytails—could also exist in literature.

the color of chocolate, whose kinky hair did not form ponytails—could *also* exist in literature.

Then I read Camara Laye and Chinua Achebe, who were a glorious shock of discovery for me. They made me begin to write stories about people who looked like me and did things that I recognized—though a few of my characters continued to drink ginger beer! *Arrow of God* was also quite important to me because it transcended literature and became personal history—I read it as the story of a man who might have been my grandfather.

I came, as an older reader, to love language, and I often reread Derek Walcott and Jamaica Kincaid for that reason. *Middlemarch* was difficult for me to finish when I first read it as a teenager, but on reading it more recently I sometimes thought that George Eliot was a version of my feminist self—her sharp, brilliant insight into gender seemed so contemporary. And *Reef* is a novel that is so beautiful in its evocation of Sri Lanka, a lost paradise of sorts, that it fills me with nostalgia for something I never even had.

Daniel Alarcón

—•• *writer* ••—

Storytelling has always been part of my family. It would have been weird if I had told my parents that I wanted to be a lawyer. Being a writer was totally acceptable. We had a lot of books in the house. I wrote my first serious story when I was sixteen. And by "serious" I mean awful, unreadable, and pretentious. My parents say that before I could read or write, I would dictate stories to my sister. She would illustrate them. And I would sign them with a *D*. One still exists. It's a story about a bean.

I wasn't prepared for Roberto Bolaño to be so entertaining. I thought his books were the kind that you *had* to read as opposed to the kind you couldn't wait to *reread*. In Latin America he is like J. D. Salinger—*Savage Detectives* is a young person's novel. And though *2666* is a much more serious undertaking, he's really doing a portrait of a generation: Latin Americans who were seventeen to twenty-five in 1973, who spread out after the dirty war in Argentina, Pinochet, and political instability, and who wandered around Europe. It's a very globalized vision of Latin America. Bolaño isn't folkloric like García Márquez; he is totally modern, urban, and sexy. In the United States, there is undoubtedly a curiosity about finding an heir to García Márquez, and he's been successful because of that. People

were very possessive of Bolaño: "*I heard about him before you did.*" I love it when people get that way about writers.

I think the essential point of storytelling—sitting around a campfire—is entertainment. Sure, it's also edification, transmission of history, culture work. But I don't think there's anything wrong with being entertaining. There's this false dichotomy between something that's literary and something that's a page-turner. And these are all books I loved reading.

I included *The Time of the Hero* for a number of reasons. One, it's Peruvian, and I thought it would be disingenuous of me not to include it. We were all raised on Mario Vargas Llosa. But I also had dinner with him in 2008, and I showed him this book, which my father had given to me. We were at this Chinese restaurant on the Upper East Side, this totally random place. The book is an early edition, it has a map of Lima on the inside, and Lima has grown so much since he wrote it. So it was interesting to watch him look at the map of the city. But he also looked at his author photo. And to see a seventy-two-year-old man look at a version of himself when he was in his late twenties—it was a really quiet moment. He was staring into his past. And he said, "This was when I was your age."

Hilton Als

writer

I wrote before I read. I liked to write down what people said, and I liked to write scripts for my favorite television shows, including *The Waltons*. When I started reading, I realized that books were connected to other people and other people's writing, and that there was this whole world of people who were connected in this vast river. It's what Jean Rhys said: "All that matters is feeding the lake. I don't matter. The lake matters. You must keep feeding the lake." I didn't know that there was this great body of water until I started reading.

I grew up in Brooklyn. My mother was more or less a single mother, even though my father coparented on the weekends. I had four older sisters and a younger brother. I think my interest in writing was spurred somewhat by my one sister who wrote poetry, a very beautiful, unique girl who grew into a powerfully idiosyncratic woman, a painter. She always made culture look so glamorous.

The writers I chose are writers who work in multiple genres. Truman Capote is inspiring in terms of what he could do with narrative nonfiction writing. James Baldwin is fascinating because he could write autobiography through different characters such as Richard Wright and Ingmar Bergman. I love Proust's ability to combine thought with narrative thrust, his ability to seemingly digress while still feeding into the scene. *In Search of Lost Time* is as much of an essay as it is a fictional narrative.

I came to Chekhov late, through a great American actress named Kim Stanley, who's no longer alive. We used to have these late-night conversations. She told me to read Chekhov. I thought the writing was boring. And she said that I had to listen to what he was saying about life, really listen. It was through his plays that I finally got into his fiction. I began to see that he was creating a universe out of whole cloth. He was creating stories about his society, Russia, in miniature. He wasn't doing these big Tolstoyan numbers. He was building brick by brick.

There is something subterranean about the books on this shelf. They have a particularly brilliant way of sending up the status quo. They let you see how politics and society worked hand in hand to create present-day writers such as Denis Cooper, Edmund White, and Adrienne Rich—people who have made a real contribution to understanding that we're different. Because the only thing writers have, really, is their experience. If I can be as truthful as possible about my own experience, then maybe it'll mean I'll join that body of water.

Paola Antonelli
curator

Il Cucchiaio d'Argento. That's my whole life. It was there when I was born. I still have it. You can see that it's falling apart, there's no more binding, no cover. This copy has all of my grandmother's notes in it. It's a cookbook, yes, but it's more of a family heirloom.

I was born in Sardinia and grew up in Ferrara and then Milan. Before I knew how to read and write, I would *pretend* to write. When I learned to read, I was so curious. My mother once caught me in the bathroom with the yellow pages. I went to school to study economics and then architecture. I worked as an architect for about five months. I hated it. I didn't have the patience. So I started working as a journalist and a freelance curator.

In Italy, good design is normal. It doesn't mean everything is perfect. But there's always a conversation about design. People have opinions. When you go to the hairdresser in Italy you find *People Magazine, US Weekly,* sure, but you also find *Domus* and *Abitare.*

Hello World is the newest book by Alice Rawsthorn, the one and only, the best design critic in the entire world. She keeps the banner of design flying high. Irma Boom designed it, and Irma is very simply the best book designer alive. I personally love reading books electronically. I proudly have a big wall of books in my apartment, but I'm continually getting rid of books that get on my nerves because I don't think they're good enough to deserve to take up space in my life. You can walk into a bookstore and find that 95 percent of the books on display might as well have been directly electronic. Mind you, they might be great texts, fabulous additions to human knowledge, but they did not need to have their own paper body. I want physical books to have a concept. Irma designs objects. Her books are breathtaking as *things.*

Since this is an *ideal* bookshelf, I've included a book I haven't read yet. *Project Japan* is about the Metabolist movement, which was started in the late sixties by a group of Japanese architects, designers, and artists. They had many great intuitions. They even thought of buildings as cells that grew together. It was a moment of great hope and great ideas for progress. I love science fiction, and that was science fiction for the real world. Rem Koolhaas is one of the authors, with Hans Ulrich Obrist. My friend Kayoko Ota produced it. Koolhaas always amazes me; he is tireless, his architect/writer/speaker/thinker's brain is always jumping. I love how he chooses his subjects. I'm dying to read that book.

Judd Apatow
—— *producer* ——

In eighth grade I read *Ladies and Gentlemen—Lenny Bruce!!* I cut out the photos and made an elaborate book report for extra credit. It was gorgeous. My English teacher, Mr. Board, claimed to have lost it, but I know he stole it and cherishes it to this day.

Part of what inspired me to read more was a road trip I took with Owen Wilson in 1997. Owen was so well read—he even knew what *The New Yorker* was! I was embarrassed that the last book I had probably read was Stephen King's *Firestarter,* when I was thirteen. He recommended Frederick Exley's *A Fan's Notes,* which I loved so much that I went on a reading tear for a few years. I remember Owen's saying to me, "I'm jealous that you get to read it for the first time." I didn't understand what he meant then, but I do now.

I chose a few books that were important to me when I was a kid dreaming of becoming a comedian. *The Last Laugh* was the first portrayal of the comedian's life where I wanted in. When I was older, I read Steve Martin's memoir *Born Standing Up.* It answered every question I ever wanted to ask him, including, "Why did you stop doing standup?" Now I have to wait for him to host the Oscars every few years in order to see him do it.

As a teenager I was really unfunny. I think I thought I was funny, but when I read what I wrote, it's really bad. I was not a great-looking kid, either. I wasn't terrible-looking. I was just good-looking enough that if I'd had a decent personality, it would've put me over the top with girls. I don't think I ever got to decent. But I knew I wanted to find a way into the world of comedy.

In high school I realized that if I interviewed comedians for my radio station, they would have to answer all of my questions. Howard Stern, Harold Ramis, Garry Shandling, Henny Youngman, John Candy—I hounded them all into talking to me for an hour. I didn't broadcast most of these interviews. I just wanted to know how to "do it." I interrogated Jerry Seinfeld once about how to write a joke, and he actually told me. Much of my success probably comes from what I learned when I was sixteen, when I tricked all those nice people into talking to me.

Everyone should read this bookshelf. You will reap untold benefits: money, fame, women, and a level of insecurity that cannot be measured by modern technology. Why doesn't that go away? I'm still looking for the book that will answer that question.

Tauba Auerbach
artist

Many of the books I chose can't be read in the literal sense—I mean, they don't have any words. _Exhaustive Parallel Intervals_ is made up of groups of numbers, for example. Josh Petherick and Christopher L G Hill's books are made out of scraps of paper and plastic bags sandwiched between clear, textured contact paper. I can't read Queneau's poems because I don't know French. The book is cut into tons of tiny strips, so you make your own poem, kind of like an exquisite corpse. I just love the structure of it.

Steven Leiber's catalogue for the Schmidt-Heinz sisters is a work of art. The Schmidt-Heinz books are themselves one-of-a kind pieces that have inspired me a lot. Steven showed them to me when I was doing research for my book show in 2011. They are glue-bound board books, and each one has different systems of alteration and content generation. For example, one has oddly angled flaps cut into each page, so that when you lift the flap, you see the page behind it, which is a contrasting color. Steven did an exhibition of these books, and the catalogue is an amalgam of all of their approaches. He used the same binding technique and the same kind of board.

Anne Collier's book is concise and beautiful. It's a frame-by-frame, page-by-page sequence of images showing a woman as she brings a camera to her eye. There is a kind of inversion wherein the reader is the subject of the artist's photo. Her gaze is so direct and straight-on. She's stalking you, and you're stalking her.

I've been an artist since it was physically possible for me to make things. It has always been the most natural way for me to engage with the world. I grew up in San Francisco, and when I was a teenager, punk music and graffiti saved me from a deep unhappiness. They also lead me to my current affection for books. I was hanging around with people who made zines with photos from punk shows, drawings, little bits of writing, or photos of tags and pieces. Although I was never good at graffiti, I was good at drawing letters on paper, so I started a sort of hand-lettered typography zine called _Twenty-Six_. I've been making books ever since.

My more recent books contain no letters at all but instead simulate blocks of stone or wood that you can flip through in tomographic slices. Others have forking, fractal-like page structures or house large pop-ups.

Dan Barber
—•— *chef + writer* —•—

My career as a chef began when I was fired by Nancy Silverton. I drove out to California after college and knocked on her bakery door, asking for a job. She made me a night baker; I worked from midnight to seven in the morning, and I was horrible. One day, I forgot to salt twenty-two hundred pounds of rosemary dough. That was the end of baking for me.

Sir Albert Howard is the father of organic agriculture; he was the first to question modern farming. In the late 1920s, he was sent to India by the British government on orders to bring Indian peasants into the modern agrarian world. He went there and realized he had nothing to teach and everything to learn. So he spent the next twenty years studying peasant agriculture in different regions of India. *The Soil and Health* is really the first book to show what an organic farm could look like, and it became a launching pad for the movement.

> *You might start to worry about the state of the world if you read these books. But I think they're all quite hopeful about the future.*

I reached out to Fred Kirschenmann when my brother and I were trying to open up Stone Barns. We needed someone to be the voice for the issues we believed in, issues encapsulated by Howard and so many of the other books on my shelf—*The Web of Life*, *Nature's Operating Instructions*, *The Lost Language of Plants*. Fred is a quiet Wendell Berry, as well as one of the largest organic farmers in the country. Even though it's hard to point to one person, he was incredibly instrumental in enabling us to do what we're doing at Stone Barns today. *Cultivating an Ecological Conscience* is his recent collection of essays, and it's brilliant.

You might start to worry about the state of the world if you read these books. But I think they're all quite hopeful about the future. Maybe not Philip Roth—*Goodbye, Columbus* is a pretty depressing book. Roth doesn't strike me as hope-filled guy.

Jo Ann Beard
writer

The first shelf I arranged was all Updike—twelve Updike books. Updike himself invited that kind of completist behavior by designing the jackets and the cases of his books so they would match, a kind of visual acknowledgment that he was in it for the long haul, beginning with his very first book. But finally I chose just two of his books. Arguably his greatest achievement was as a short story writer, but Rabbit Angstrom—his conservative politics and weird misogyny notwithstanding—is especially dear to me, so much so that when I read the account of Rabbit's death in *Rabbit at Rest,* I felt my own heart stop. That I might run from him in so-called real life but have an endless appetite for his shenanigans in the novels is, of course, testament to Updike's magisterial skills as a writer.

> *That book, in a moment of dialogue, taught me a lesson about allowing the reader to meet me halfway.*

Sometimes books can have a tremendously helpful effect on a writer. While reading Tom Drury's *The End of Vandalism,* for example, I felt something shift in my approach to my own work. Good literature is a collaboration between reader and writer, and that book, in a moment of dialogue, taught me a lesson about allowing the reader to meet me halfway.

I was given *My Friend the Dog* when I was a girl, and it was probably one of the happiest reading times of my life. My mother got it at a yard sale and eventually collected the whole series for me that way. On the front of each book there is an engraving of a collie—what could be more beautiful?

To answer that, look at *Junkyard Dogs and William Shakespeare.* Mark Lamonica is a sculptor who spends a lot of his time going to junkyards to look for material. He's also a photographer, and he photographed the dogs he encountered, then further ennobled them with quotes from William Shakespeare. Be prepared to cry when you read it.

Jen Bekman

curator + entrepreneur

When I opened my gallery, it was a total departure from everything I'd done in my career—I didn't have any training or background in art. The decision was an impulsive one, prompted largely by my irritation that nobody had ever tried to sell me art. It wasn't the realization of some lifelong dream, but it's a path I'm glad I followed. When we opened our doors, in 2003, my driving mission was "art for everyone," and it still is.

I initially connected to art through the worlds of design and architecture. I'm a longtime admirer of the work of Ray and Charles Eames, and I've been profoundly inspired by their "design for everyone" ethos. They were about accessible yet smart design; a joyful, playful inventiveness; and the creative use of unconventional and high-quality materials. I mean, wow, talk about innovation! And look at how enduring their impact has been.

I like to think that *Eats, Shoots & Leaves* approaches grammar in a way that's similar to how we try to help people live with art. So many people are intimidated or bored by grammar, but this book engages with it in an easygoing and fun manner. It shows you the craft of language without making it feel like work. I've always taken a similar approach to talking about art: you don't have to get all fancy and use highbrow language to validate that a work of art is interesting or good.

I read *Ways of Seeing* in media studies when I was in college, and it's stuck with me ever since. Berger writes about how reproductions of the *Mona Lisa* have only strengthened the iconic value of the original painting. I'm very much on board with that idea. Scarcity continues to be one of the primary drivers of value in the art world, but I'm a firm believer in access and the power of building an audience. I'm a huge champion of prints and multiples: I always say that the artist's editions we're selling at 20x200 enhance the value of the limited-edition works, rather than diminishing it. It's been satisfying to see that assertion proved true as the business has matured.

I came to realize over the years that there was no way to reach the public on the scale I envisioned through just a physical location. It seemed natural, given my Internet background, to extend the idea of "art for everyone" online, and that was the thinking that led to the creation of 20x200. What started out as a wacky idea has now evolved into a multifaceted endeavor. Sometimes I look around and wonder how it all happened, but mostly I feel like we're just getting started.

Coralie Bickford-Smith

book cover designer

When I was a teenager, I got expelled from college. My father marched me in to see the deputy head, who read me a William Blake quote that has stuck with me ever since: *He who binds to himself a joy / Does the winged life destroy. / But he who kisses the joy as it flies / Lives in eternity's sun rise.* College was a struggle. My parents had forbidden me to study graphic design. But when I eventually made it back to college, my art teacher said that some of my work looked like William Blake's. Blake illustrated, colored, and printed his own books. I started a project about him, and it got me a place at Reading University to study typography. I see my love of Blake as my way into design.

When I began working at Penguin, I found a Web site that showed all of the H. G. Wells covers that had ever been published. I couldn't imagine what I could bring to the world of cover design, as it seemed all to have been done before. And I respected that. Over my first year, I kept thinking about what I could do as a designer.

Could I find a way to make people love and cherish books without subverting the essential values of a Penguin paperback? Penguin was founded in 1935, when Allen Lane was returning to London after a weekend's visit with Agatha Christie in Devon. He was at a train station, and

he wanted a book to read—something inexpensive but engaging. But the selection was dreadful, nothing beyond popular magazines and reprints of Victorian novels. So he invented Penguin.

Nowadays there is an abundance of cheap books to read. But I still wanted to think about the book as an object, as something passed down from generation to generation. I became obsessed with bookbinding—Art Deco bookbinding, Victorian bookbinding—which led me to think about how materials such as cloth and foil, alongside quality printing, could add a really beautiful finish. Which is how I came up with the Cloth Classic series. The pattern I created for *Dracula* is composed of garlic flowers. In the book, the heroine wears garlic flowers around her neck to stop Dracula from biting her in her sleep. So the idea is that they're wreathed around the book, too, to keep in the evil.

I love the fact that I get to repackage amazing literature that has stood the test of time. I really couldn't be designing anything more important. The written word means so much to me. If I design a cover that gets people to pick up a book, then I've done my job. I want the younger generation to fall in love with books like *Jane Eyre* again. That's why I do what I do.

Mark Bittman
—•→ *journalist + cookbook author* ←•—

I never had an office job for more than six months—and even that was very nearly thirty years ago. Every time I took a job and walked into an office, I would break into a cold sweat as soon as I got there. I wanted to write; I always wanted to write. But I think I wasn't good enough at it to make a living until I merged it with cooking. I probably wasn't good enough at cooking to make a living at that, either, but the combination of the two seems to have worked for me. Since then I've written about pretty much anything that appealed to me or, sometimes, to my editors.

> *If you knew me, you'd know that each of these books is a part of who I am.*

I often question whether I'm all that creative, though some people flatter me and insist I am. In any case, I've created this odd and pleasing and rewarding career for myself. A lot of what I do is instinctual, and it's more craft than art: yes, my job is creative, but it's got well-defined boundaries. That's what being a journalist is like.

If you knew me, you'd know that each of these books is a part of who I am. That's true. When people say things like "I want to be Mark Bittman" or (for example) "I want to be Jonathan Lethem," what they're really saying is that they want to have a career like mine or his. They don't mean they want to have my house, my habits, my wife, my children, or my parents—and that's what this stuff is about. It's the personal side of things, not the professional, which is why I can honestly say that I read all of these books for pleasure.

Sophie Buhai & Lisa Mayock

fashion designers

SOPHIE: Kenneth Anger's *Hollywood Babylon II,* which I found at a Salvation Army store, is my favorite book ever. I bought eight copies to give as gifts. It's like the original *US Weekly*—in it you'll find all of the most scandalous tales of Hollywood from the twenties and the thirties. With whom did Mary Pickford have an affair? How was Douglas Fairbanks caught in a scandal? I have a lot of nostalgia for Deco Hollywood. Fitzgerald was writing during that time, as was Tennessee Williams. You can see that influence in Vena Cava's graphics and silhouettes.

Man, Myth, and Magic is this very rare occult encyclopedia that my friend got me on eBay—it was published in the late sixties and contains everything you want to know about the occult. I find it fascinating to read but also fascinating to look at. It references a lot of ancient Egyptian and New Age symbolism, both of which themes inspire our prints. The floating triangle that you often see in occult books has become a recurring motif for us.

LISA: I think I've recommended *The Game* more than any other book. Every single guy I know has read it. It's an understood thing—they've all read it, and they will never talk about it with women. Neil Strauss is supposed to write about this pickup artist named Mystery. Strauss is a total nerd, bald and not particularly good looking, but Mystery takes him under his wing and turns him into a very successful pickup artist. The book is part how-to, part narrative—and the techniques are incredibly manipulative but successful. I think it's a fascinating insight into a man's brain. And it's a fun read.

Even if I'm being slightly facetious about Neil Strauss, I do think all of these books take you into their own worlds. *The Elegant Universe* does that quite scientifically. *The House Book* does it in a very literal way. Reading is not unlike that moment when you go into a thrift store: there's always this element of chance, where you don't really know what will be there and what you'll find. You might stumble upon a pink letterman jacket and think it's really cool. And maybe you'll discover that you love wearing pink letterman jackets for the rest of your life. It's an opportunity to create a new self. These books do that, too, I think.

Rosanne Cash

→ *musician + writer* →

I read *The Diary of Anne Frank* as a teenager, and it was the first time I began to think about oppression and the horror of war. It was an unknown world, and it transfixed me and awakened my nascent sense of righteousness and social justice. When I was sixteen, my dad took me to Amsterdam, and we visited Anne Frank's house. I realized with a shock that she had lived in a room the size of a closet. It was so much smaller than I thought it would be. Her diary really helped to develop an adult-sized compassion in me, something I had only a vague awareness of before reading the book.

I think books find their way to you when you need them.

When I was younger, I sought out books. I was one of those kids who asked my mom to drop me at the library on Saturdays. That was where I spent my weekends. In a childhood that felt chaotic and unsafe—with all the anxiety of having a father who was a drug addict and a mother who was enraged about it—the library was my refuge. I loved being there. I felt safe in the library and with the librarians. I felt that I was valued and that my passion for reading was a good thing.

But my father had magnificent books. Ancient books. Do you know the writings of Josephus? He was a first-century Jewish-Roman historian. My father had an early nineteenth-century edition of his work, and it was amazing. My dad would get so anxious if anybody held it, if anybody touched it. He loved books more than anything. Whenever he traveled and he had time off, the first thing he would do was go to a used bookstore. And I remember doing that with him when I was a teenager. I'd travel with him, and whether we were in Dublin or in Alabama, we'd find a used bookstore. That helped me develop a real love of books—not only for reading, but as objects in themselves.

I think books find their way to you when you need them. Whenever I feel like I'm not going to live to read all the books I want to read, I remind myself that the important ones find their way to me.

Michael Chabon
— *writer* —

In 1982 I wrote a story for my undergraduate fiction workshop, and my teacher told me it reminded him of Borges. I had barely even heard of Borges, but I immediately rectified the situation and got hold of *Labyrinths*. I discovered a kindred spirit. He was a writer who was clearly first and foremost a reader, whose writing unabashedly, almost obsessively reflected his passion as a reader. And since writing starts with reading for me, I recognized a sympathetic mind on the page. I loved his offhand creation of entire fictional universes. He has the effortlessness of a great athlete who can do the things he does on the field without really thinking about them.

I read Barthelme that same year. That was a big year for me. It was a time when I was porous to experience, as we all are at nineteen or twenty. You're very open to trying all kinds of new things—experimenting and dabbling and putting yourself out there. I was acutely interested in writers and their styles. Anything I wrote was an imitation of whomever I was infatuated with that week.

But that was how I learned to write, and it's the approach I recommend to people who want to write. It's through imitation that painters learn to paint and composers learn to compose. It is an incredibly useful way to figure out how to write like yourself in the long run. And it's much easier and more pleasurable to imitate a writer whose work you love.

I can definitely see strong echoes of Fitzgerald in my first novel, *The Mysteries of Pittsburgh*. I can hear that I was reading a lot of Proust; I can hear that I was reading Cheever. I can especially hear Cheever in the short stories that I wrote around the same time. I don't think it was until *Wonder Boys* that my voice really began to assert itself. I'm not Grady Tripp, but his voice is my voice. I hit on it with my very first sentence. I wrote the first draft in seven months.

But it has never really occurred to me until this minute why that was so easy for me to do: it was because I had finally arrived at this synthesis of all those influences. You can detect echoes of Chandler and Pynchon, and there's a certain amount of the literary game-playing you might find in Borges. There's also a very conscious allusion to works of genre fiction by such writers as Lovecraft. It's all there. Your style is still going to be constructed out of the material that you have inherited, but it's going to be put together in some way that has, hopefully, never quite been heard before.

Candy Chang
—•→ *artist + urban planner* ←•—

I was a bright-eyed college student browsing the shelves at the local bookstore when I came across *Letters from the Avant-Garde*. It's a compilation of stationery designed by artists of the Bauhaus, Constructivist, De Stijl, and other design movements. I took it home, and it became my design bible for the next few years. Whenever I felt stuck, I'd flip through those pages. The Modernists' use of white space, grids, and bold type helped stir my own iterations, and I learned the fundamentals of good design by remixing their approaches. The way I stumbled upon this book also made me forever appreciate the serendipity of bookstores and libraries—of picking up anything that catches your eye. The world becomes more rewarding if you let yourself look beyond what you're searching for.

The world becomes more rewarding if you let yourself look beyond what you're searching for.

Some books on this shelf mark turning points for me. I was a designer at the *New York Times* when I happened to catch an episode of *New York: A Documentary Film* on television. I watched the whole series and bought the book.

I became infatuated with the history of the city. I learned about Robert Moses, who planned to bulldoze a swath of lower Manhattan to make way for a ten-lane highway. And I learned about Jane Jacobs, who got the members of her community so worked up that they prevented Moses's highway from being built.

It's shocking to think how different New York would be today if that highway had happened. The "slums" that Moses wanted to clear out are now some of its greatest neighborhoods: the West Village, SoHo, Chinatown, Little Italy, the East Village, and the Lower East Side. It made me think about all the cities that could have been and the cities that we have now, depending on who got or gets involved. That's when I decided to leave my job and study urban planning.

Whenever I get tense, I spend time with Antoine de Saint-Exupéry and E. H. Gombrich. They both say profound things in simple, humble ways. The first chapter of *A Little History of the World* is called "Once Upon a Time," and it's a poignant reminder of our place in the expanse of history. When you think about your life in the context of the beginning of the sun and the sea, that deadline next week will suddenly be put in its place.

David Chang

⬗ *chef + cookbook author* ⬗

This is sort of a lending library. It's what we keep in the bathroom at Momofuku Ko, which sounds funny, but it was literally because of space constraints. The goal was to have a bookshelf that we could reference, that we could point to for inspiration at the end of the day. It's a shrine of people we admire. And a lot of these cookbooks are ones you can't find at Barnes & Noble—though I've taken the more rare books out of circulation. The best ones tend to get stolen.

In many ways, this bookshelf is like a collection of baseball cards.

We call people who we admire in this profession "ninjas," which is why *Ninja* is on here—I'm not sure anyone's actually read it. Olivier Roellinger is inspiring because he's a chef who stumbled upon a culinary career—his life story and his work with seafood are incredible. I guess it's our way of being able to keep current with what happened before us. Without a chef like Thomas Keller, we wouldn't be here. I love his books. *Bouchon* is on here, but I couldn't risk losing my first edition of *The French Laundry*, which I think is an iconic book. It'll be around forever; no other American cookbook has encapsulated a chef's philosophy better than his.

My favorite books are probably those I can't even read—they're in Spanish, like the el Bulli book. That's really an encyclopedia of food. In many ways, this bookshelf is like a collection of baseball cards. There are some chefs on here that I don't even really refer to when I cook, but it's more out of respect. I think what they've done is cool. Not every player is your favorite, but some are rare and more meaningful in strange ways than others. You still collect them all.

LA ALTA COCINA VASCA EN MINIATURA · Pinchos y Picas · Ed. Gourmet Press

Préparez TERRINES, FOIES GRAS ET SAUCES à l'école des professionels · Éditions St-Honoré

The Big Fat Duck Cookbook · Heston Blumenthal

essential cuisine · MICHEL BRAS · Laguiole, Aubrac, France · ici La PRESS

COCO · 10 World Leading Masters · 100 Contemporary Chefs · Φ

el Bulli 1983-1993

6 (sei) · AUTORITRATTO DELLA CUCINA ITALIANA D'AVANGUARDIA

FEARNLEY WHITTINGSTALL · THE RIVER COTTAGE MEAT BOOK · Ten Speed Press

La cocina del restaurante Kursaal Martín Berasategui

JAUME COLL · EL CELLER DE CAN ROCA, UNA SINFONÍA FANTÁSTICA

Elkar · CICEM · • The Professional Charcuterie Series · Cottenceau Deport & Odeau

Flammarion · Christian LEJALÉ · ROELLINGER · Trois étoiles de mer

The Forager's Harvest EDIBLE WILD PLANTS · SAMUEL THAYER Forager's Harvest

bestiarium gastronomicae · Gyula Madarász Andoni Luiz Aduriz José Belmonte Rocandio · 111

NGUYEN · Into the VIETNAMESE KITCHEN · Ten Speed Press

DICCIONARIO BOTÁNICO PARA COCINEROS & Andoni Luis Aduriz Françoise Crattolinger Sánchez

MARLEY · Mushrooms for Health · Down East

Olivier Roellinger's Contemporary French Cuisine · Flammarion

sergio

JEAN-GEORGES · JEAN-GEORGES VONGERICHTEN AND MARK BITTMAN

WINDOWS ON THE WORLD · Complete Wine Course · STERBE

UN RECORRIDO POR LA HISTORIA DE MONTAGUD EDITORES (1906-2006)

WWW.QUIQUEDACOSTA.COM

MARTEKA MUSHROOMS: WILD AND EDIBLE

BOUCHON · Roger Vergé's Vegetables in the French Style · THOMAS KELLER · ARTISAN

Joel Levy · Ninja the Shadow Warrior · M · ARTISAN

STEPANOVA LIUBA EUTNEV

SHOCKING LIFE Elsa Schiaparelli

LEANNE SHAPTON THE NATIVE TREES OF CANADA D&Q Petits Livres

THE PATHFINDERS THE EPIC OF FLIGHT/TIMELIFE BOOKS

TOILE DE JOUY RIFFEL ROUART WALTER Painted Textiles in the Classic French Style

COHEN

SONIA DELAUNAY ABRAMS

Dressed for the Photograph Ordinary America and Fashion 1840-1900 JOAN SEVERA

TRAPUNTO by MACHINE Hari Walner C&T Publishing

BARRATT LOGIC & DESIGN Design Books

Claire McCardell · Redefining Modernism Yohannan and Nolf

Pioneer Women Peavy & Smith Oklahoma

The Quilts of Gee's Bend Tinwood Books

ART DECO AND MODERNIST CARPETS Susan Day

TEXTILES OF THE WIENER WERKSTÄTTE 1910-1932 Angela Völker

Native Funk & Flash

The Pile Weaves Jean Wilson Scrimshaw

MODERNIST JEWELRY 1930-1960 The Wearable Art Movement Van Cort and Reinhold Schiffer

Schon

SEVEN ARROWS HYEMEYOHSTS STORM 351-00-0

HUMAN DIMENSION & INTERIOR SPACE by JULIUS PANERO AND MARTIN ZELNIK WHITNEY

Soft Jewelry Design, Techniques, & Materials Howell-Koehler

HULL POTTERY · Roberts

A Second Treasury of Knitting Patterns by Barbara G. Walker Schoolhouse Press

YES YOKO ONO ALEXANDRA MUNROE JON HENDRICKS

Hannah Höch album HATJE CANTZ

Anne van Cutsem A World of Head Ornaments Skira

Rachel Comey

fashion designer

I didn't understand the vast world of fashion until my late twenties. I studied sculpture and printmaking throughout school. I was never the child who pored over the pages of *Vogue* and dreamed about glamour. If anything, I was interested in textiles, hardware, unusual materials, shapes, proportion, but then also streetwear and cultural trends.

Studying art was my first step into that world; it pleased me to work in three dimensions. Later I learned that the fashion industry had so many exciting facets to it, that the challenge of being a designer and manufacturer would be constantly stimulating. The craftsmanship, the entrepreneurialism, the manufacturing process, the production cycles, and the pace—all of those things really appeal to me. It just took me a while to figure that out.

When I was first starting my own business, it was all blind ambition. I was totally naive. I called up friends, and friends of friends, and they modeled the clothes for me. It was cute. I was lucky in many ways. I started my business on credit cards and naiveté. You know how credit card companies send you a free offer—you can have an interest-free card for sixty days? I kept opening new accounts and transferring balances. It was a bit risky, but I discovered I was really good at it.

I got really into fashion history during my early days of designing. I find Claire McCardell inspiring. She had such a modern point of view. Look at the clothes she made. You just know that if her garments were in production today, many would still be spot-on. And I try to think about that. My brand has a practicality to it that I might attribute to her influence, but it's also quite different—a bit funny, playful, hopefully relevant and beautiful. I try to make sure that aesthetics, rather than getting in the way of the wearer's day, will instead enhance it.

I collect books; this shelf is more of a reference library for me. Until I came across *A World of Head Ornaments* at the Strand, I never really thought about them. I might look at that book to see how to make a piece of hardware on a shoe, or a closure on a garment, or even a print motif. Sometimes I look at books of early photos, like *Pioneer Women,* for styling. In fashion, you spend about six months designing a collection, but it's only around show time that you finally begin to put it all together. You have maybe six weeks to think about the looks, the hair, the makeup. Before that it's all about shapes, colors, prints, stitches, textures, and so on. Show time is when I turn to some of these books.

Robert Crais

writer

I grew up in Baton Rouge, Louisiana. In those days, if you told people you wanted to be a writer, they thought you were either joking or strange. Everyone did real things. That's the way it is in most of America—you're an accountant, you're a lawyer, you're a doctor, you're a police officer, you're a fireman.

I read everything I could get my hands on. The only reason I picked up *The Little Sister* was that the cover had this really hot chick on it—that was all I needed at fifteen. I'd never heard of Raymond Chandler. But reading that book planted the seed for my fascination with Los Angeles and began my love affair with detective fiction.

Back in the sixties and seventies, Harlan Ellison wrote a column for the *Los Angeles Free Press* called "The Glass Teat." It was about his adventures as a television and movie writer in Hollywood. We didn't get the *L.A. Free Press* in Baton Rouge—I guess it was considered too radical—so I used to drive down to New Orleans once a month to buy it. When I had about half a dozen short fiction sales under my belt and was starting to feel that maybe, just maybe, I had a modicum of talent, I left Louisiana for Los Angeles with the crazy dream of becoming a television writer. Ellison's book made this seem like an attainable goal.

I think of my television years as an education, even though I also went to the Clarion Writers' Workshop. Writing for *Hill Street Blues, Cagney & Lacey,* and *Miami Vice* taught me an enormous amount about dialogue, pacing, editing, and characterization. It was like a very intense graduate program. As I shifted my career from scriptwriting to writing novels, and then as those novels began to sell, what I'd learned from television played a large part, I'm certain, in my literary success.

Robert A. Heinlein wrote science fiction, and his work gave me a true appreciation of the loner hero. Invariably his protagonists were kids from nowhere, with no advantages, who somehow pulled themselves up by their bootstraps and overcame all obstacles. I identified with those characters as a teenager. I felt like an alien beamed down from the *Enterprise*. In *Stranger in a Strange Land,* Valentine Michael Smith is literally a Martian: he's a human being, but he was born on Mars. And Heinlein, who was himself a Naval Academy graduate and former engineer, always had a very powerful message in his stories: Work hard, stay focused, be creative, be smart, and you can succeed. This was an important life lesson for me, and I took it to heart: Don't give up.

Sloane Crosley

→ writer →

I grew up in a literate but not particularly literary household, which I think is significant. My dad reads the *New York Times* every day, but there're a lot of *National Geographics* and a lot of Robin Cooks on the shelf. He spent some time in Ireland, so we had James Joyce. That's about it. My mom is a huge book-club reader—give her a copy of *White Oleander,* and she'll be done with it by the next morning.

They were very encouraging of my creativity, but I never thought that I could make a living as a writer. They did give me *The Best American Short Stories of the Century* after I studied abroad in Scotland. I was in love with Edinburgh and really did not want to come home. But I felt as if I had no free will and I most certainly had no money and so home I came. This book was waiting on my childhood bed, with the inscription, *Welcome back to America, we missed you.* It was such a lovely reminder of my country: "Stay here, you know? It's not so bad. We made you this thing called a Flannery O'Connor, what else could you want?"

We don't tend to think of humor as a skill; instead we talk about it as a gift. But I don't believe that certain individuals are born funny and thus simply grow up to be funny people, any more than I believe that I could decide, say, to become really good at physics and wake up tomorrow as a physicist. So there is this implication afloat that humor comes naturally, and it does. But it doesn't mean it always comes out flawlessly. A good humorist works on improving his or her craft. There're a lot of crap diamonds. I know when I've oversaturated a paragraph with them. I know on a very technical and boring level when I need to insert a beat in the midst of all the jokey stuff. The question is, do I make a move to fix it? The answer lies in the difference between writing a bad short story and a bad comic essay: when you write a bad story, you're an otherwise okay person who's written a bad story; when you do bad comedic writing, you're just not funny.

Even though Annie Dillard's *The Writing Life* is the slightest book on my shelf, there's a quote from it that I like to repeat: "Aim for the chopping block. If you aim for the wood, you will have nothing. Aim past the wood, aim through the wood; aim for the chopping block." That's the trick for how you're supposed to write, humor especially. Don't look it directly in the eye.

Adrian Danchig-Waring & Pontus Lidberg

—•• *dancer + choreographer* ••—

ADRIAN: My body chose ballet. My mother says that when I was a baby, I had dancing toes. As soon as I could, I started moving. My first ballet teacher gave me a copy of Robert Henri's *The Art Spirit* when I moved on beyond her teaching capabilities. I am always trying to put my dancing in the context of an art practice as opposed to a job, an athletic pursuit, or an interpretive skill.

I'm not much motivated by dance biography. There isn't a huge value for me in trying to model my own path after those taken by the heavyweights of ballet. But there is a lot to learn through understanding how artists have channeled their experience into their practice.

PONTUS: I chose two photography books for the same reason. Both the Francesca Woodman and the Duane Michals were gifts from a friend when I was seventeen. Different art forms and aspects of life itself inspire me more than other choreographers do. I admire other choreographers' work, of course, but these two books in particular inspire me to create.

ADRIAN: I think we're both influenced and inspired by mediums other than our own. We're looking for that moment, any moment, when you witness great art and the execution of mastery. When I stand in front of a Rothko

painting, for example, it inspires me to use my medium—which I suppose is my body—with masterful strokes.

PONTUS: The thing about dance, and ballet, is that you can't expect fast results. It's something you have to pursue regardless of the weather.

ADRIAN: That's really counterintuitive because there is always this perceived endpoint. The body can do these things for only so long. I think it's a matter of finding some sort of grounding throughline amid all the insanity, which these books do. I think of Alice Waters's book as a bible. It's a testament to purity of form, of flavor. And it's grounding to me because it doesn't have the same baroque trappings that the ballet imposes. It's important to find a way to enjoy simplicity in the face of everything else.

PONTUS: There's a really good mix on this shelf, from art to life to love to food.

ADRIAN: I think, to be perfectly honest, these books are less a true representation of myself and more a reflection of the person I want to realize.

PONTUS: Well, I think I chose books that get at the essence of who I am.

ADRIAN: That's what I'm saying, too, but I think I'm not there yet.

Tom Delavan
interior designer

When I read *The Ice Storm,* I felt that it was my childhood come to life—I grew up in Connecticut in the seventies. I remember watching the movie and thinking that Ang Lee had totally nailed it. Everyone was embracing that slightly dysfunctional modern aesthetic. There's a part that still makes me laugh: Sigourney Weaver's character is walking out of her house in heels, and she slips. The reality of their lives doesn't match the stage they've created for themselves.

I ended up in interiors very circuitously. My first job was at Goldman Sachs, as an analyst doing leverage buyouts. I just got it wrong; I was working seven days a week at something that didn't inspire me. I didn't really know what I wanted to do. I had friends who worked at the Factory, and at *Interview,* and that world really intrigued me. Andy Warhol seemed so central to social life in New York. If you were at party and he was there, you were like, "Oh, good, I'm at the right party." *The Warhol Diaries* remind me of that time when I was trying to figure things out.

There are books here that taught me about space. Donald Judd was an artist whose work was inseparable

To me, nothing is more beautiful than a wall of books.

from architecture and design. He bought this old fort near Marfa, Texas, and created these amazing environments that let you see how art can live and define a space. And I love Cy Twombly. What I find appealing in his work is the balance between disorder and order, between color and whiteness. But he also lived with art in a beautiful way. My favorite interiors are his. There are these famous pictures by Horst of Twombly's house in Rome; it's so clear that an artist lives there. He has these beautiful antiquities alongside his furniture, stacks of paintings, and everything else he could need, and it all flows together. It's not one of those places where someone has hung a really expensive painting alone on a wall and it feels like a gallery. Art was an integral part of his life.

Books are the very best kind of decoration, really. There are two types of books, the ones you read and the ones you have on your coffee table. Both make a space feel like home—you spend time with them, they have meaning for you, and they actually look good, too. I have clients who tell me that they don't need a library because they do most of their reading on an iPad. It makes me sad. To me, nothing is more beautiful than a wall of books.

Junot Díaz

writer

Immigration first got me reading. I arrived at six years old, in 1974, in central New Jersey. At the time, the United States was a profoundly hostile environment for immigrants. We're talking about a United States that had just emerged from a catastrophic war—more catastrophic for the Vietnamese than for the Americans, though you wouldn't know it. Reading provided a number of reprieves. It provided a harbor.

In reading, no one could criticize my English. In reading, I could practice English; I could live in English. It's like when you're learning to dance: God forbid you go to a club where there's a competition going on. That was really what it felt like to learn a language when and where I did. Books, too, were an enormous revelation to me. I had come from a family and a place in the Dominican Republic where books were basically medieval—few people had them, and they were very precious. The United States was a country of books.

I wish I could summon my younger self to explain why I fell in love with *The Lord of the Rings,* because the person who falls in love is not the person who remembers falling in love. I'm like a forensic investigator trying to put the pieces back together. But I think it was the way Tolkien created this extraordinary, secondary world, and how, through that, he enchanted the primary world. That resonated with me. His books had power to transform what we otherwise take for granted. Reading *Lord of the Rings* made me see how a novel was another world— and see that I could immigrate there, too, whenever I wanted.

These books show that I'm trying to understand the world. I'm trying to understand what it means to be an American in what we would call the long American century. I'm very interested in that. For me there's always the wonder of how closely we can exist under such impossible odds, the wonder of a new life brilliantly told. But despite how romantic and sentimental I am, I don't think you can be an American without reflecting on the role of U.S.-sponsored torture in the world. You can't be a person of African descent without thinking about the struggle against white supremacists. And those books are here, too. That's how you build a healthy identity that isn't propped up by forgetting, by erasure, by avoiding, by negation, by denial.

Simon Doonan

→ *writer + fashion commentator* ←

I was born in England during the fifties, when the country was still recovering from the war. It was very grim, very black and white. And in the early sixties, a scrappy working-class woman named Vivian Nicholson won the football pools. Reporters stuck a microphone in front of her, asking what she planned to do with the money, and she said, "I'm going to spend, spend, spend!" She immediately embarked on this catastrophic spending spree, every moment of which was documented in the press. We couldn't wait to see her self-destruct, which she did very publicly.

I'm very committed to the notion of bad taste. Good taste is an illusion.

She bleached her rock-hard beehive, got a poodle and dyed it pink, and drove up and down her old street in a Cadillac convertible. She eventually became penniless. My sister found her memoir in a used bookstore and gave it to me. For me, Nicholson's life is a cautionary tale about money: if you live in abject poverty and want out, you need to make sure it's on your terms.

I love Iris Murdoch's *A Fairly Honourable Defeat* because of the way she writes about homosexuality. To her, it's not a big deal. The issues are the same: you're born, you get sick, you have medical insurance, you die. I was gay when it was illegal, when it was classified as a mental illness. And I had a lot of anxiety about that because everyone in my family was out of his or her mind—both my grandmother and my uncle were schizophrenic. But eventually I realized that being gay was my ticket out. I'd get on a train to London and go to a gay bar, and suddenly I was mixing with people from all the social classes. Being gay was what we had in common. As a gay man, you can transcend socioeconomic boundaries faster than anybody else.

I was fortunate enough to see Liberace perform in Las Vegas in the late seventies, and it was dismal and spectacular all at the same time. He was such a strange self-creation—he even paid his boyfriend to have plastic surgery to look like him, and then they wore matching snow-leopard coats. I'm very committed to the notion of bad taste. Good taste is an illusion; it's an oppressive construct designed to make us feel wretched about ourselves. I put *The Things I Love* on my shelf because Liberace is a heroic figure for me. Go for it, I say. Life is short. Why shouldn't you have rhinestones glued all over your Rolls-Royce?

JUDITH KRANTZ *Scruples*

IRIS MURDOCH *A Fairly Honourable Defeat*

MARY KARR THE LIARS' CLUB

the Idler book of CRAP TOWNS B@XTREE

TOM WOLFE THE PAINTED WORD

CAMILLE PAGLIA SEX, ART, AND AMERICAN CULTURE

The Custom of the Country EDITH WHARTON

SPEND, SPEND, SPEND Vivian Nicholson & Stephen Smith

Vidal Sassoon Sorry I kept you waiting, madam

The Things I Love *Liberace*

Jennifer Egan

— *writer* —

I knew I wanted to be a writer by the time I had read most of these books. But in each case, they made me think, "Wow, you can do *this*." Even though I don't feel a direct sense of influence—I would like to have been influenced by these books, but I'm not the best judge of whether I really have been—I am always inspired. I'm reminded of what a novel can do.

I think about *Tristram Shandy* and *Don Quixote* all the time. All of the innovations that have come since in the novel are foreshadowed or outdone by these authors. Their books are so playful, authoritative, and strong. It reminds me of how flexible the novel form is and what it's capable of doing. I derive strength from these books.

Emma has always been my favorite Jane Austen novel. A lot of people tend to like Emma—she's such a winningly flawed person. One thing that surprises me about Austen is that her characters are very inflexible; nobody changes that much. Emma might be the slight exception, but she still stays Emma in the end, even if she's a little bit wiser. You could almost say that Austen deals in types, which normally is a very dangerous practice and doesn't lead to anything interesting. Yet her

work is stupendous. Her novels work themselves out with a tremendous clarity that feels mathematical or geometric. It's very spare; there's nothing extra. Her books shouldn't work, but they do, and better than almost anyone else's.

Middlemarch is great in all of the big nineteenth-century ways, offering lots of minor characters who become very interesting, a huge canvas, a very complex world. If you compare Eliot to Dickens—who is another favorite of mine—what's great about *Middlemarch* is that there is never any sentimentalism. She's emotionally controlled.

In Dickens, there's a visible self-indulgence, especially around suffering boys. *Middlemarch* doesn't have that, but emotionally it's still a wrenching book to read. Eliot's portrayal of a sexless marriage is devastating. She never gets out the violin, tempting though it may be. I admire that.

My goal as a writer is to do as much as possible at one time. Life itself is so cacophonous and complex. It's not that I want to create a cacophony, but I want to do justice to the complexity around us. I don't want to oversimplify it. I want to take one thing and build from that, and then keep building, until I begin to approximate the complexity of the world and our perceptions of it.

My goal as a writer is to do as much as possible at one time.

Dave Eggers

—— ⤞ *writer* ⤝ ——

It surprised me to realize how dark so many of these books are. Sorry about that. My main goal was to limit the choices to those books that have hit me hardest. That was the only criterion: each book had to have made a huge impact on me when I first read it. I left out books that I loved at one time but am not as connected to now, and I ended up with this, a shelf of books that overall have some fairly dire subject matter.

These are the books that crushed me, changed me when I first read them, and to which I've returned many times since, always finding more in them. I really am the kind of dork who goes back to the same books for inspiration again and again.

More than any other book, *Herzog* is what I turn to when I need to be reminded of what's possible. I can open it to any page, begin reading, and feel an electric current shoot through me. It makes me feel alive to the possibility of what can happen on the page, what can happen even in one sentence.

Same with *Lolita*. For most of the last ten or fifteen years, I've kept copies of *Lolita* and *Herzog* next to me when I write. Not that there's much evidence of Bellow's or Nabokov's influence in my own writing, hard though I tried to imitate them both awhile back.

The rest of these books are the ones I push on other people. People ask me what they should read, and I tell them that *The Known World* is the best novel of the last twenty-five years, that Edward P. Jones is our contemporary Steinbeck. I tell them that everybody always forgets that Sartre was a great novelist, and that they should start with *Nausea*. I tell them that Lorrie Moore was the first contemporary writer I sought out in every week's *New Yorker,* and that her writing, along with early work by Didion, enabled me to get through my young adulthood with my senses and hope intact. I tell people that Vollmann's *Rising Up and Rising Down* is the best primer on the history and justifications of violence. I tell people that *For Whom the Bell Tolls* is by far Hemingway's best work, and that *Jesus' Son* is short, funny, impossibly lyrical, and a book that no one doesn't like. That *A Star Called Henry* made me believe again in the epic novel. That no one has written a better existential novel, filled with dread and possibility, than Bowles did in *The Sheltering Sky*. And finally, I tell people about *Travel Writing* by Peter Ferry, an excellent novelist and my high school English teacher.

Tina Roth Eisenberg

⟶ graphic designer + entrepreneur ⟶

I started my blog because I needed a personal visual archive. I'm Swiss, so I'm neat and organized, but I can't remember a name for the life of me. I needed something visual, with lots of images. You have to understand that this was before Tumblr and all of those other visual bookmarking sites we have today. I'm often asked what it is about design and Switzerland, and I think the Swiss have this inherent desire to organize things, to keep them orderly and neat. I am not surprised the grid system came out of Switzerland. I like to joke that the Swiss have an extra gene for order that other nationalities don't have. We expect things to be well designed, well thought out, and well done. When you grow up with such a mindset, surrounded by beautiful, clean design, it sure has an impact on your aesthetic.

I think it's very important to see beauty in the ordinary. And for whatever reason, we've lost that eye.

My parents were entrepreneurs but not exactly creative types. I caught the bug from my Aunt Hugi, who's a fashion designer and this very eccentric, free, creative soul.

I was eight or nine when I learned about graphic design from her partner, and from that moment on I knew that was what I wanted to do with my life. I would join student clubs in high school and college just so I could make the posters for them. I did it all by hand—this was before computers. It's actually really crazy to think about that now.

A lot of the books I've chosen are related to design, typography, and visualization: works by Edward Tufte, Lars Müller, Paul Rand. What's interesting to me about Rand is that he was not only an amazing designer but also a fantastic communicator. Most designers are good at expressing themselves through shapes, colors, and type but struggle to eloquently explain why they do what they do. Paul Rand is the big exception; he had a brilliant mind.

Taking Things Seriously fuels my obsession with the seemingly mundane. I think it's very important to see beauty in the ordinary. And for whatever reason, we've lost that eye. A designer who can restore that sensibility can make a quality product. By stripping something down to the bare minimum, the truly essential, a designer inevitably conveys a more powerful message. It's not easy to do, but it's important to try.

Merrill Elam & Mack Scogin

— *architects* —

MERRILL: In high school, there was a day when firemen and doctors came in and talked about their careers. There were two architects in my hometown; one of them came to my school and advised us absolutely not to become architects. He said it was the worst job imaginable. It involved a lot of worrying, and you could never make any money at it—he went on and on. Of course, that didn't discourage me at all.

The most battered book on my shelf is *A History of Architecture on the Comparative Method,* by Sir Banister Fletcher. We were required to buy that during our freshman year. That's my original copy. It's a history of architecture around the world and then some. The book predated color photography as a norm in reference books, so it's illustrated with just these black and white photographs and line drawings of all the great European buildings. I still use it. If I want to know the exact dimensions of Saint Peter's, I look in that book. I can Google it now, but for years I couldn't. So that little book is a real treasure. It was our beginning.

MACK: Merrill and I met on our first day of architecture school at Georgia Tech, in 1961. Merrill was from Clarkesville, Tennessee. And I was there because Georgia Tech was the only place I could afford to go: if you were in-state, it was very inexpensive, just ninety dollars a quarter. I don't think you would have called either of us especially worldly. My parents took me up to New York City one time when I was a kid, but that was about it.

But there we were, both enrolled in architecture school. There was a professor who taught the history of architecture—using the Banister Fletcher book—but he also took it upon himself to teach art history. And Merrill and I were both in that class. The professor had a fantastic art collection, unbeknownst to us. One day he showed up with two paintings wrapped in brown paper; he was carrying them under his arm. And one was a Francis Bacon self-portrait. The other was Salvador Dalí's *City of Drawers.* He simply unwrapped them and showed them to us. I'll never forget looking at the Francis Bacon—I'd never seen anything like that before. All I could think was how there was so much out there that people were seeing, that they were seeing differently, that I would never experience. I still think this. Seeing art like that for the first time was a life-changing event for me. And I think for Merrill as well.

Derek Fagerstrom & Lauren Smith

LAUREN: I think this shelf represents a little bit of everything that we're interested in. We chose some books for their obvious aesthetic appeal—the brick cover of the Conran book, the beautiful Jesus Bug from *The Principles of Uncertainty*. You crack open Bill Owens's *Suburbia* and it takes you into this whole world that perfectly captures the time and place where we grew up in northern California. The colors in Margaret Kilgallen's drawings are so inspiring, as are those in the Alexander Girard book. We just got rid of our television and sometimes, for entertainment, we'll each grab a stack of art books and flip open to a page—just to discover something we haven't seen before.

> *We just got rid of our television and sometimes, for entertainment, we'll each grab a stack of art books and flip open to a page—just to discover something we haven't seen before.*

DEREK: The bookshelf represents the span of our attentions and affections—art, home décor, old-fashioned adventure. We're not one of those couples with floor-to-ceiling design books or photography books. We have all kinds.

We always try to keep our minds and eyes open, which sounds ridiculous, but it's true. We try to surround ourselves at The Curiosity Shoppe with as many interesting, fun, and smart people as possible. It's contagious.

The Curiosity Shoppe is our design store and gallery in San Francisco. The name comes from a group we started in New York, where we'd meet every month with our friends. Each time, someone was responsible for teaching everyone else something new. Lauren taught knitting and crochet; one friend taught us how to play a card game; another friend in the wine business taught us how to taste and order wine.

We called it a Curiosity Guild—it was a play on the Learning Annex. I loved the idea of the Learning Annex but there was never something there that I wanted to take or see. This was our way to get together with friends and teach each other things in a way that was slightly more productive than going to a bar and drinking. Curiosity is a driving force in our lives. We're both big believers in curiosity.

Drew Gilpin Faust
— historian —

I found myself drawn to books that I had assigned in classes, often multiple times. The influence these books have on me is in part a reflection of the influence that they may have had on a generation or more of students whom I had the privilege to teach.

Absalom, Absalom! is one of the great American novels—and perhaps the greatest to depict the American South and the Civil War, the focus of my teaching and research. The book is on one level a meditation on what history is and why it matters. But it is also a story of Quentin Compson, a young Mississippian of the early twentieth century who is struggling to come to terms with the legacy of race and oppression that is part of his heritage as a white Southerner. He must understand the past in order to distance himself from it. We cannot create better worlds until we comprehend the world we need to abandon.

A number of the books on my shelf are about wars other than the Civil War, because I found that my writing and teaching required me to consider a broad context. *The Great War and Modern Memory* is a classic study of the changed consciousness introduced by the slaughter of the Western Front. *Dispatches* and *The Things They Carried* represent equivalent transformations of human understanding initiated by the war in Vietnam. These books all provided insight for me into the power of war's impact on human minds and cultures.

My father was in Patton's Third Army, landing in France just after D-Day. I have a photograph of him on the steps of Notre Dame at the time of the Liberation of Paris. I think it was the high point of his life, and it made me, by influence and inheritance, a Francophile. This is partly why I love *Le Petit Prince* and decided to include it here.

There is a notion articulated by the little prince regarding the need always to destroy the bad plants—*arracher les baobabs,* in the original French—that grow around us before they become so large as to overtake us. The prince notes that it is best to do this "at the very first moment when they can be distinguished from the rose-bushes which they resemble so closely in their earliest youth." I continue to think of that. We must constantly *arracher les baobabs*. That is what Quentin Compson is attempting to do, in part, as he undertakes his exploration of the roots that entangle him. In almost every one of these books, it is always somehow about roots—about history, that is, and about how we confront and transcend it.

James Franco

—◆— *actor + writer + artist + filmmaker* —◆—

Tony Hoagland was my first serious poetry teacher. He introduced me to a lot of the poetry here. For three years, I read *Tar* over and over again. I liked it so much I acquired the rights to it. I adapted the first poem from Frank Bidart's *Golden State*. I made a film about Hart Crane based on a biography called *The Broken Tower*. It's new territory for me, though in no way am I the first to do it.

I try to choose narrative poems. It's not as if I'm adapting Wallace Stevens. Part of the challenge is to identify the tone. A poem can point in many directions at once. It isn't under the same kind of pressure to produce anything specific. A person or a place can stand for many things at once. When you shoot a film, well, now, you choose a location, you cast your lead. If you wanted, you could shoot in ten locations with ten different actors for one scene, but it'd be a mess.

My father gave me *As I Lay Dying* when I was fourteen. I loved it—the structure, the style, but also the characters. I'm so used to learning about people through conversation, and this book is a great example of how you can understand character so differently. I thought *As I Lay Dying* was like a puzzle. For me, as a teenager, it was much more difficult to figure out what Faulkner was trying to do—so it became a mystery I was obsessed with, something I wanted to unravel. I think turning a book or a poem into a film is a similar process.

L.A. is a film city, and that was calling me the loudest. I wanted to go to art school, but my parents wouldn't pay for it, and so I went to UCLA instead. Because I didn't apply to enter the UCLA drama program as a freshman, I was going to have to wait until my junior year to apply; two years felt like a lifetime to me. Granted, I was eighteen, so who knows how clear my thinking was, but a degree seemed like a ton of work. I wanted to do art, I wanted to write, and I wanted to be an actor. So I left. I put all my energy into acting, and it paid off. But eventually I realized that I still had all these other interests. I was writing and reading, but I didn't show my writing to anybody, and I didn't really talk about books with anybody.

The crossover of mediums and disciplines is something that really interests me; I think it brings energy to the other projects I do. In some ways, I've learned not to run from my identity as an actor or as someone involved in a lot of things. I've actually learned to embrace that.

Sasha Frere-Jones

writer

I especially enjoy reading anyone who isn't writing on a critic's schedule. As a columnist, I'm always too aware of time. Reading John Jeremiah Sullivan, who digs into subjects over time with a very particular voice, is a good example of that kind of pleasure for me, as a reader. But it's also sustaining to read an earlier critic like Otis Ferguson. Ferguson doesn't have the same cachet as someone like Edmund Wilson, because he died in action at thirty-six during World War II. He was skeptical and enthusiastic and—while I don't have any illusions that people from the Golden Age were better writers or thinkers—he embodied the voice of a certain moment. Reading him is inspiring in a familiar way, specific to the gig. There's no reason to think a deadline is an excuse to give the work your left hand.

There's a writing hangover in the family tree. My great grandfather was Edgar Wallace, who wrote a zillion crime novels, and then came up with the story for *King Kong*. I didn't know what that meant as a kid. I thought *King Kong* was a corny movie; by college, I had realized it was this gross racist parable. I wanted to forget the whole thing at that point, and I was playing in a band full-time, so I was able to. I was more impressed with my grandparents. My grandfather was the chairman of William Heinemann, and my grandmother wrote for *Tatler* magazine. They were exactly what a kid from Brooklyn would imagine of English people—incredibly dry and funny, using vague references to all sorts of people I didn't know.

Being a writer was the first job I thought I might be qualified for. (I let go of first baseman dreams early, which was uncharacteristically pragmatic of me.) In high school, writing meant plays, and in college I wrote decent poetry and cultural theory that predates the Internet and is lost to the sands, thank God.

I was in a band long before I became a critic. Playing music blocked out the sun for the writer in me: my mind needed to organize ideas in a sort of all-consuming visual way (my clumsy mode of composing), and my hands had to do things other than type. I wrote in notebooks, but my focus shifted away from words for almost ten years. I didn't write anything even close to an essay or narrative story. That's part of why I feel a bit like a visitor as a critic. I don't come to the discipline from within the discipline. I love the conceptual challenge, though. The heart of the game is hearing something, tracking its movement, and trying to figure out what, exactly, the music is doing.

Tobias Frere-Jones

typeface designer

Our dad worked in advertising on Madison Avenue. I discovered typography by tagging along with him on the weekends. I would wander down the hall and into the office of someone who'd just quit or been fired. I swiped those expensive markers with the precisely calibrated ink; I got my first type specimen book out of a garbage can in the art department.

AT&T was one of my dad's clients. He went out to the company's intergalactic headquarters in New Jersey, and when he came back, he told us how the engineers at AT&T would build a phone and throw it out a second-story window to see if it would still work afterward. They called it the drop test. I thought that was inspiring—the idea of putting all that care into something and then deliberately abusing it to see if it would survive. We do a lot of that in type design, drawing something and then seeing if it will survive at 5-point. But I remember my father's saying that the folks at AT&T took their job so seriously that they actually had their own special alphabet drawn for the phone book. *What?* That was like telling me that someone designed water or customized air. What he was describing was Bell Centennial, which Matthew Carter drew in 1978. I remember looking at the phone book and seeing that

indeed, the letters were different in there.

I used to stare at my Rand McNally atlas for hours. I would do these tracing-paper experiments. I remember really enjoying the shape of Cyprus—have a look at it on a map; you're not going to mistake it for anything else. It was like playing "name that tune" using just the first three notes: if I could render a shape in six straight segments and still have it "read," as it were, as this country or that landmass, then I knew I had accomplished something.

The one thing a type designer needs more than anything else in the world is patience. Having a command of the historical scholarship is great; having the technical chops to get through lots of increasingly complicated stuff is also great. Drawing skills you can pick up. But patience can't be substituted for, particularly with the tools we use now. But if you open up a copy of *Specimens of Printing Types Made at Bruce's New-York Type-Foundry* and look at a lowercase *e,* just imagine having to sculpt it at that size in reverse at the end of a bar of steel. That's what these guys did every day. It was an insanely time-consuming process, but there was actually a hidden benefit in that sort of effort: it gave designers a chance to reevaluate, rebalance, and polish a little bit more.

Ben Fry
—❧ *data-visualization artist* ❧—

It took me a long time to get into reading. I had a first-grade teacher who was particularly meanspirited and prone to dole out guilt trips to the class when we behaved poorly. I wound up in the slower reading group. Eventually I pulled out of it—the story my parents tell is that one day I came across one of my father's engineering textbooks, which had been put in storage out in our barn. I was completely enthralled by the diagrams and shapes and other complex things on its pages. And my parents told me that if I learned to read, I could read books like that. I can't say for sure that that was what got me reading, but I quite vividly remember looking at that book. It's funny now to think that I haven't changed one whit in terms of the things I like to look at and think about.

Our design studio is called Fathom, which actually began as a Mark Twain reference. Twain got his pen name from "two fathoms," which is the depth of water required for a riverboat safely to navigate a channel. The young Samuel Clemens would sit on a riverbank and listen to the crewmen on the boats yelling out "Mark one" (for one fathom) or "Mark twain" (for two fathoms). I'm amazed by Twain's ability to use very simple language to express really complicated ideas, or humor to convey a serious

point. Too much of visualization work seems to consist of making one complex thing explain another, significantly *more* complex thing. I think it's important to execute an idea with simplicity and grace. That's what I love about Tim Hawkinson's work, for instance: he's able to put a notion of space or quantity into a perceivable volume or mass through his sculpture.

I've always been interested in design, data, and programming, but for years, I believed they were separate pursuits. In grad school, I was able to mix these interests in a way that made sense: I could do design but use programming as a means to open up new avenues for the complexity of issues that I needed to address.

Instead of just designing a simple train schedule, for example, I could also design an underlying system that would take into account how the schedule would change every few months. This approach is not about making design somehow automatic or any less human; it's about recognizing the fact that data is continually changing. Code gives you a way to master the evolution of data over time, so you're not just stuck with a static snapshot of the data, as is the case with more traditional information design.

Rivka Galchen

⤙ *writer* ⤚

I started by reading the sides of cereal boxes, the Subaru manual in the car, and the few very random books that we had around the house, none of which were for children. My family wasn't particularly into buying books, or magazines, either, though we did get the Israeli newspaper delivered in the mail—but even that would arrive about ten days late. In some way, I think that lack was operative in making reading seem so wonderful and private a space, one full of almost scrutable information. Words like *riboflavin* still kind of excite me.

Words like riboflavin still kind of excite me.

The Good Soldier Švejk and *Catch-22* both belonged to my father. *Švejk*, from my dad's point of view, was mostly about the brilliant maneuver of pretending to be an idiot. *Catch-22* was maybe a more manic and complicated exploration of the same theme. It would be nice to think that these books were somehow part of the story of my life, if only because then, whenever I am being foolish, I could comfort myself by thinking that maybe I'm just playing the fool. Both books have my father's underlining of the words that he looked up in the dictionary (English wasn't his first language), and the first few words on the first few pages kind of haunt me: *anabasis, hepatitis, chaplain*. I think they, too, might make for a life's story.

I'm not sure how these books define me; I just love them. Maybe what the books have in common is that they all seem to be by thinkers who take life seriously enough not to be straightforwardly serious. And there's the feeling here of a kind of bacchanalian festival of . . . rationality. If you read them all, perhaps you would feel as if you had attended a large variety of tea parties.

Atul Gawande

—• *doctor + writer* •—

I never thought I'd become a doctor/writer. I read Lewis Thomas's *Lives of a Cell* as an undergraduate and was completely captivated by Thomas's way of thinking in completely literary terms about science. I felt the same about Oliver Sacks: he saw not only the science of the tiny mechanisms at work in all of us but also the whole human beings that we are.

The Doctor Stories is a collection of factual pieces by William Carlos Williams about his life as a doctor in Paterson, New Jersey; the stories themselves are incredibly vivid and revealing. And *A Farewell to Arms* is some of the best writing there is about medicine. The novel is set in a tiny hospital in Milan. The narrator is injured and falling in love with his nurse, but the simplicity of the story masks the complexity of what Hemingway is trying to do, of the many layers he's capturing: history, doubt about one's place in the world, dignity.

When you're the son of two Indian doctors, as I am, you're supposed to become a doctor yourself. It's what everybody expects you to do. And it's natural that you should feel somewhat resistant to fulfilling those expectations. I hoped that I might become something else along the way.

It was definitely not my plan to go into surgery. But when I got into the operating room, I just *liked* it. I liked the atmosphere. I loved the sense of the possible. Even the blood and guts. Being a surgeon means grappling with risk and uncertainty but also having to make good decisions under imperfect conditions. In a way, it reminds me of the job of a political leader, who has to consider complex information, make difficult decisions, take action (because any action at all is often better than inaction), and then live with the consequences.

There was a time in college when I tried to write short stories. I also tried to start a band. I wanted to make an impact. But I had nothing to say. Eventually I disregarded that impulse. I make an impact as a doctor, as well as with my research and public policy work. But as a writer I don't feel that way. Writing is about speaking to others who may be confused about the same kinds of things that I'm confused about, and who are willing to follow along as I explore what's interesting to me. How else would I end up writing about itching? I just wanted to tell a story. And I hoped it would make people feel really itchy when they read it.

Malcolm Gladwell
→ writer →

I'm in the middle of writing my new book, which is about power. I'm very interested in the strategies we use to keep people who are powerless in check. And the ways in which the powerless fight back. So I started reading about crime. I've probably acquired 150 books just for this project. I haven't read all of them, and I won't. Some of them I'll just look at. But that's the fun part. It's an excuse to go on Amazon. The problem is, of course, that eventually you have to stop yourself. Otherwise you'll collect books forever. But these books are markers for ideas that I'm interested in. That's why it's so important to have physical books. When I see my bookshelf expanding, it gives me the illusion that my brain is expanding, too.

For a while I was interested in whether there was something to be learned from crime stories. If you think about organized crime and the way in which the drug trade is treated today, you realize that as a nation we're incredibly punitive. But back in the forties and the fifties, we turned a blind eye. I started to read crime memoirs to get a sense of what it was like to experience the great penal experiment that began in America in the seventies. Most of these memoirs—*On the Rock,* for instance—are weirdly unselfconscious. They're oddly revealing. This is storytelling by people who aren't professional storytellers. That's always much more useful to someone like me.

Francis A. J. Ianni is really cool. In the fifties and sixties, he was granted amazing access to a very prominent mafia family in New York. He changed everyone's name for publication, though I'm sure that someone could figure out who these people really were. I found his account riveting. It's not the *Godfather;* Ianni is a sociologist. But he makes you think about the role crime plays in the domestication of ethnic minorities, and whether crime rates are a necessary stage by which those minorities enter the mainstream.

The problem with crime is that it's so depressing. There's no good news. *Texas Tough,* for example, is totally fascinating, but when you read what we've done with our criminal system over the last twenty-five years, it's the saddest story in the world. I want to tell some of that story in my book, but I can't do too much because then it'd be unreadable. I don't think I'm capable of writing a book about depressing subjects and making it interesting. I need the subject itself to be reasonably uplifting.

Kim Gordon

artist + musician

I remember reading D. H. Lawrence as a teenager. I have an older brother, so I'd often pick up what he was reading. There's so much sensuality in Lawrence's writing, which really appealed to me—and I don't exactly mean the sexy scenes. Anaïs Nin has it, too. I was a shy kid. We lived in Hong Kong when I was thirteen. It was a city with a free port, and there were sailors everywhere. It was very weird to be ogled by sailors at such a young age. I remember that my mother was always trying to get across the idea that "if you're pretty, boys will like you, but if you're smart, they'll like you longer." She was terrified by the fact that I looked older than I was. I remember being so selfconscious, but I think I understood that I had a certain power as a *jeune fille*.

I found Alan Watts in the late sixties. I wasn't quite old enough to be a hippie, but I was interested in different forms of rebellion. There were psychedelics around because of my brother. I had a friend who was very political, more political than I was, and we'd check out demonstrations together. I didn't attend the last semester of high school because there was a teachers' strike, and we wanted to support the teachers. It lifted me out of the doldrums of being a teenager. My brother had a friend who referred to me as a weekend hippie, which hurt my feelings. But I'd

be curious to read Alan Watts again now, in light of the Occupy movement.

The Lonely Doll is a children's book. There was something about that doll, the bears, her clothes, that Upper East Side apartment, everything—the book provided me with my first image of a New York interior, in a way. I read it as a kid, and years later, I couldn't remember who'd written it or think how to find it. Then Thurston Moore found someone on the street selling a mockup of the original, bought it, and brought it home. I remember being so excited to rediscover that book. In 2004, someone wrote a biography about the author, Dare Wright. A lot of women have talked about how that book influenced them, including Cindy Sherman and Anna Sui. I tried to read it to my daughter, but it was too strange. It's a sick little book.

I always wanted to be an artist; playing music was something I fell into as an escape. I thought it would be interesting to make art and comment on it from within. Of course, Sonic Youth wasn't very mainstream. Our ambitions were really small: "Well, let's get a gig at CB's." "Let's put a record out." "Let's go to Europe." We didn't know what we were doing. Which was kinda fun. We just wanted to do *something*.

Philip Gourevitch

writer

I'm mostly aware of what I'm leaving out. But looking at this shelf is like looking at some of the key building blocks in my brain. The minds of these authors are all quite wild. They have huge scope. They're fearless. Except perhaps for the bird guide, all of these books grapple hard with what it means to exist and to confront the universe.

There's a deep American vein here, too. There's Ralph Ellison, who directly and indirectly—sometimes hilariously and often furiously—tackles race, that core American story. There's Melville, who goes out to sea, goes a-whaling. He makes Ishmael's voyage physically immediate and metaphysically infinite at the same time. And you can hear Melville in Ellison, but Dostoevsky, too. So these books don't just speak to me, they speak to each other.

Photography fits right into that conversation. Robert Frank shot *The Americans* on a single cross-country trip in the fifties. You can enter into it as you would a collection of stories. Or I should say it enters you—and you learn to recognize Frank's way of seeing with the same particularity as you recognize a voice over the phone.

Naipaul, from Trinidad, is also a writer of the Americas. *In a Free State* has a story called "One Out of Many," about a Bombay servant named Santosh, who accompanies his boss to the United States. It begins: "I am now an American citizen and I live in Washington, capital of the world. Many people, both here and in India, will feel that I have done well. But . . ."

By the time I was a teenager, I knew that books like these were the company I wanted to keep. I started out writing fiction and took up reporting later, when I was in my late twenties. Reporting is the only work I've ever loved as much as writing. They're really separate activities: one is about going out into the world and taking it all in, and the other is about sitting in your room, drawing the world back out of yourself, and putting it down on paper.

This shelf is mostly fiction, because novels taught me how the world works—or at least how to think about how the world works. Fiction and nonfiction both have to be true, but nonfiction has to be fact-checkable as well.

However, imagination is a great reporting tool. Imagination enables the reporter to ask better questions and collect better stories. It also reminds us that reporting isn't merely telling other people's stories; we need to ask, too, why those stories are *our* stories. If I'm telling stories in a way that somehow makes them inescapably yours, then I guess I'm doing my job.

Jorie Graham

⤛ poet ⤜

I chose this shelf arbitrarily when I was asked for it, grabbing whatever I could find that day, as if I were about to be hit by a hurricane. Today I would perhaps have a different list—an absolute need for Proust, Beckett, Milton. If I were stockpiling for the end of time, I might choose quite differently indeed!

In this gathering, I put some of my essential poets. Eliot and Dickinson should be there but are missing. Among the other volumes, J. Hillis Miller taught me a great deal about how to read: I still go back to him to be reminded about the plain old right relationship between the search of the poet, his or her vision, and its embodiment in form, style, and architecture. Not much fussy theory there, just really close reading.

The Structure of Verse was assigned to me, in an earlier edition, by my teacher Donald Justice when I was a student at the University of Iowa. I am never without it. And I never open it—especially the essay by Jespersen—without feeling for a split second that I am back in my third-row seat in his classroom.

Death & Friends was written by another one of my teachers, now deceased, the wonderful, relatively unknown poet Jon Anderson. It was one of three books he wrote

as a graduate student at Iowa. It's taught me more about syntax over the years than most books of verse. Otherwise, the lessons in syntax come from Virginia Woolf, Henry James, William Faulkner—but I did not think it would be that long a hurricane, or I would have grabbed *Between the Acts,* as it is my most essential prose book, alongside *To the Lighthouse.*

Regarding the nature of poetry, Coleridge says it "brings the whole soul of man into activity." I take this to refer to what, for me, is its essential characteristic: its capacity to put your whole body in contact with a form of absolute mystery without making you feel afraid. Poetry "resists the intelligence almost successfully," as Wallace Stevens puts it. No other art in words does quite the same thing, though music does, and the visual arts can as well. This is why poetry is more often aligned with the latter two mediums than with prose.

As to what I would say to a young writer? Don't think of it as a career, think of it as a practice. Read everything by one poet. Learn one whole language and world at a time. Don't worry about understanding it critically. Not at first. Not for a long time.

THE STRUCTURE OF VERSE Edited by HARVEY GROSS ECCO

Death & Friends

HENRY VAUGHAN THE COMPLETE POEMS YALE

BATE John Keats OXFORD GB 166

JOHN ASHBERY SOME TREES CORINTH M

Pearce

When the Rivers Run Dry WATER—THE DEFINING CRISIS OF THE TWENTY-FIRST CENTURY BEACON

Marianne Moore Complete Poems MACMILLAN VIKING

THE COLLECTED POEMS OF WALLACE STEVENS ALFRED A. KNOPF

rainer maria rilke THE COMPLETE FRENCH POEMS Translated by A. POULIN, JR.

FIELD NOTES FROM A CATASTROPHE Elizabeth Kolbert RILKE graywolf

MILLER Poets of Reality Belknap Press Harvard

Elizabeth Bishop The Complete Poems

YOUSSEF WITHOUT AN ALPHABET, WITHOUT A FACE graywolf

James Merrill Poems 1946–1976 From the First Nine Atheneum

William Carlos Williams Selected Poems NDP

ZBIGNIEW HERBERT REPORT FROM THE BESIEGED CITY

Andrew Sean Greer
— writer —

Whether I like it or not, it turns out that these are the books I turn to in a panic. I used to open *Lolita* up at random, for instance, just to challenge myself to set the bar a little higher; the writing is so exciting and dense, full of jokes and wordplay. And while I'm not sure *Rebecca* is an endless source of wisdom, there is something mysterious in the telling, the long distance of memory, that inspires me. You have to admit it's got a beautiful cover. In fact, Jonathan Lethem gave it to me—he's a book maniac, as we should all be.

And now my secret: everyone in the world is a better reader than I am. I used to be ashamed and would pretend to have read books or authors I hadn't heard of, but I don't do that anymore. I read as a writer, not as a critic. I've been reading *Lolita* and Proust almost every day for a decade, if you can believe it, looking for ideas; I have finally forgiven myself for not reading everything in the entire world.

And these are the books I steal from. There's a crazy part at the end of *The Chateau* in which William Maxwell has a Q&A with the furniture—I love that and stole it for a story of mine, and I regret nothing. Nothing! It turns out that Maxwell himself stole it from *The Marble Faun*! We don't write in a void. Our storytelling comes from reading, learning, and trying out techniques we love. As Pound says, we ought to have either the decency to acknowledge a theft outright or the cleverness to hide it. Since I can't hide anything, I guess it's clear where I stand on that point.

I think if I made a shelf to impress, it would look different, but this is a writer's shelf. And you know what? Now that I look at it, I think, God, it looks gay! Maybe not to the untrained eye, but c'mon: Frank O'Hara, William Maxwell, Colette, and, of all the Graham Greene to choose, *Travels with My Aunt*! I might as well have put down *Auntie Mame*. It's funny to me that somehow I've never been pegged as a gay writer, for better and worse. I've actually been taken aside by other writers and told that I'm a bad gay—that my gay characters aren't triumphant enough. Blame it on Colette! I just don't think of fiction that way at all. I would be all for propaganda if not for the fact that it doesn't work—everyone always knows what it is. There is none of it on my shelf. I like books that ask questions and that perhaps have no answers. It's a tough line to walk. But it's the same one any writer walks, with the same goal: to make something that no one has ever seen before.

Lev Grossman

I had two formative periods as a reader. The first was when I was eight to twelve years old and read works by fantasy writers such as C. S. Lewis and T. H. White. It's difficult to say what it was in particular that I responded to, but those are melancholy books and I was a melancholy little boy. I suppose I thought or believed or hoped that there was another life waiting for me in Narnia. Then, in college, I took a course on the modernists in my freshman year. We read Woolf and Joyce and Hemingway, and I felt as if I had been waiting for them my whole life. They confirmed everything that I suspected was wrong with the world. These books have stayed with me for the rest of my reading life.

I always wanted to write novels. But I was the opposite of a *wunderkind*. I took so many false steps. I don't think there was a single word that came from my genuine self until I was thirty-five. I was in the middle of working on a novel when I read Susanna Clarke's *Jonathan Strange & Mr. Norrell*. And I remember I stopped typing because I realized I'd been looking in all the wrong places. So I started over again. And it was a different kind of writing than I had ever done before—faster, more enjoyable. I had forgotten that it didn't have to feel like breaking rocks. Of course, I had to spend four years revising *The Magicians,* and that felt like breaking rocks again. But it was a different rock this time, and a much more precious ore.

Watchmen is a really important book to me. It did for superhero stories what I hope to do with fantasy. At some point, superhero stories began to feel very exhausted. *Batman, Superman, Spider-Man:* it was just the same stories over and over again. Even if you loved them, you were sick of them. And Alan Moore was obviously sick of it, too. He was trying to think seriously about what kind of person would put on close-fitting tights and beat up muggers. Who would do that? What would have to be wrong with somebody who chose that life? And what effect would it have on anybody who had to do it night after night? He went right for that. He depicted superheroes as being neurotic and washed up and angry and sociopathic. It was astounding. By attacking all the sacred beliefs of the superhero story, he wrote the greatest superhero story that I've ever read.

I spent a lot of my writing life being rejected. I always tell people to never, ever give up. Because one day you'll have that moment, and you'll start writing real words in your own voice. It might take longer than you ever, ever imagined it would, but it will happen.

Gabrielle Hamilton

—➤ *chef + writer* ➤—

My parents got divorced when I was thirteen. I started working in a kitchen right away. And I ended up getting trapped there. Once you start doing something and you get better and better at it, suddenly there's your whole life in front of you. It can go that way. It was going that way for me. For a long time, my kitchen work was my excuse for not writing. I can't go home and write, I'd think: I just worked an eighteen-hour day and now all I want to do is drink and smoke.

Now that I do both, it's funny: I find that I'm the same in writing as I am in cooking. They work differently, of course, but in tandem they create a whole. I approach writing the way I do hospitality: I'll provide the food and the table. I'll clean up. And you eat.

Of Human Bondage by W. Somerset Maugham was a pivotal book for me. I was eighteen; I was lost. I had dropped out of college, possibly twice. I was deep into an existential angst that was beyond cliché: What the fuck are we doing on this planet and why do we have to be here? The opening lines of that book go: "The day broke gray and dull. The clouds hung heavily, and there was a rawness in the air that suggested snow." What a grim tale. But my own days were gray and dull. And it was the perfect book for me at that particular point in my life. It did exactly what only a book can do, if you're ready for it. It met me where I was. There is no better experience.

Everyone asks if I read food writers. And I don't. Improbably, it's John Berger whom I always keep at the top of my mind when I have to write about food. I don't like food writing because it's so fetishistic and nearsighted. Berger would never write about Bordeaux wine. It would just be wine. It's bread, it's cheese, it's wine, it's soup, it's berries, it's milk from the cows. And all the while, he's not writing about soup at all; he's writing about, you know, rural poverty.

I think all of these books give the reader permission to break the rules. I included the Bible not for religious reasons but because every sentence in it starts with the word *and,* which every teacher always tells you not to do. Of course, the greatest lesson is to know what the rules actually are. And *then* you can break them. I'm pretty certain you can't reverse the order. Jackson Pollock could draw a very fine figure and e. e. cummings obviously knew correct syntax and grammar. You can't start out using all lowercase letters and no punctuation. You have to know all the rules first. Then you can play.

Daniel Handler

writer + musician

I used to go to the library each week and check out a different book by Zilpha Keatley Snyder. And then one day they didn't have any more that I hadn't read. So I thought, I'll give her a week off. I came back two weeks later and there was still nothing. I was so irritated. How long could it take? And then I remember discovering *The Changeling* in the bookstore. I almost had a heart attack. I bought it and read it to tatters.

I started writing for children because someone asked me to. I thought it was a different skill set, even though it's really not. I asked the editor to send me a bunch of children's books that the publishing house had published. And they were all terrible. Every single one of them. Which inspired me.

I was afraid to reread Roald Dahl when I was starting out. I had enough of him in me already.

I love *Danny the Champion of the World*, but I was afraid to reread Roald Dahl when I was starting out. I had enough of him in me already. He sees the world as being both absurd and terrifying. You never have one without the other in his work. *The Bears' Famous Invasion of Sicily,* however, uses a tone that I ripped off for Lemony Snicket.

The voice is erudite but useless. It's supposed to be omniscient, but it doesn't know everything. It worries. It's philosophically digressive. I also find it amusing that my guide to writing for children was somebody who had never written for children. Dino Buzzati was actually a fairly well known political writer in Italy, as well as a goofball novelist.

I read Baudelaire in sixth grade. I must have thought *Flowers of Evil* was a horror novel. It was the first time I had ever read any poetry that seemed rebellious. And I liked Baudelaire's whole attitude. For me, at that age, it was a pose: "The world is shit, and everybody who says otherwise is a liar. All I want to do is wander through the streets, gazing at the stars and drinking a lot." I thought that sounded fantastic. It doesn't sound good to me anymore, but it sounded great then.

I was seventeen when I read *Self-Help.* Lorrie Moore was writing about situations that weren't superfamiliar to me, but they were familiar enough. In high school, you're mostly reading *Madame Bovary.* And Lorrie Moore introduced me to the idea that literature could be about the things that were around you. She was tangible. She was alive and well. It felt like she was right there.

Tony Hawk

⤏ athlete ⤏

I picked up *A Child Called "It"* in a bookstore because I remember my mom's mentioning that it was the worst-ever documented case of child abuse. It's shocking to think about what happened to the author, but I find it an incredible story of overcoming adversity. It's more amazing that he was able to take what happened and turn it into a positive victory.

Endurance is about a ship's crew's fight to survive under the absolute worst conditions imaginable: they were stranded on drifting ice packs in Antarctica for half a year. The book is a lesson in what human beings are capable of; it shows that when things are at their worst, you always have to keep going, you have to keep trying. It's about perseverance. In Shackleton's case, it was the perseverance to stay alive. For me as a skater, it's the perseverance to succeed—not necessarily in order to beat other people, but just to do it for myself. Just to know that if I set my mind to it, I can do it. It might have taken me years to get this one trick, but it's worth it to know that I can do it, even if someone else had already done it before me.

Punk has always been very closely intertwined with skating, which is why I put *Please Kill Me* on here. I heard my first punk concert at a skate park. I remember it was

in L.A., I was really young, and my brother had taken me there. And all of a sudden, all these punkers started swarming—the Dead Kennedys were playing there that night. I already knew the music from hearing it around. I liked the energy, the do-it-yourself vibe, and it was very much in line with what was happening in skating. I grew up on punk rock as much as skating.

I think a lot of the books on this shelf are about pushing the boundaries of the mainstream. How can you be successful by doing something else? And I think you might be able to see from these books why I'm so determined, why I was able to overcome the adversities I faced in trying to make a career out of skating. Because skating was not something that was encouraged or supported at all when I was young. But I didn't really care if I was financially successful. I wanted to do it so much.

For me, skating is my escape, my outlet for creativity. It's as much of an art form as it is a sport, so I really love the freedom it gives me, and I love the control I have when I'm doing it. And, of course, I love the adrenaline. The feeling of landing something for the first time—it's that rush I always strive for. Still, to this day.

Todd Hido

photographer

Photography gave me an outlet. I think making art gives you an opportunity to sort out your feelings, to explore what you often can't explore in any other way. Every one of us has a story to tell, and sometimes we don't even know we're telling it. Fortunately, earlier in my life, I was around people who fostered my self-expression, among them Larry Sultan. His book *Pictures from Home* is on this shelf. He taught me to draw from within. He also made me think about how I could approach sentimentality without becoming sentimental.

What I love about Edward Hopper is the mood, the atmosphere he creates. There's this universal longing for connection that I see in his work, and it's something that I've always admired and tried to emulate. Diane Arbus cuts through all the bullshit, basically. She's so utterly in your face, so undeniably real. And there's a sexual element to Nan Goldin that I admire—it's not a territory you can ignore, you can't turn away from it.

I can see a synthesis of all these people in what I try to do in my own work—there's atmosphere from Hopper, there's realism from Arbus, frankness from Goldin, and a sense of interiority from Larry Sultan. For me their books are strangely autobiographical, in a way.

The Contented Little Pussy Cat is a children's book. I'm also interested in pulp fiction: *The Sinful One, Sexology,* and *All Legs.* I don't think I've read more than a page of any of them. I like them because of their covers, their titles. Books are like that. You're looking at a book called *The Sinful One,* and on the cover there's a picture of a very suburban blond woman, and that makes you want to pick it up. And that's why those books are on this shelf. They're there purely for the possibilities they represent.

I think it's important to spend time looking at books—physical books. I love the Internet, and there's no question you can find really interesting work and photography on Tumblr, for example. But a book allows you to see someone's work completely. Photography is such a specific medium; a book might just be the very best place to view it, even better than an exhibit.

There are exceptions, of course—Andreas Gursky, for one. I make big prints, too, and seeing them in person is a very different experience. But in most cases I really do find photography books ideal, uncompromised somehow. And I think it's extremely healthy for anyone who wants to be a photographer to look at real objects. Spend three hours at the Strand bookstore. Get out there and look.

Pico Iyer
writer

Nobody, I hope, could make a pattern or find a thread among the few books on my tiny shelf here in my two-room home in rural Japan. Each speaks to a different mood, a singular period in my life—an alternative me, in effect. Each is like a friend who arises from a parallel universe in my past. There's the old school pal who's been hanging out with me, each of us arresting the other's development, since we were fifteen; there's the pure, quiet soul I met in a monastery once; there's the one I encountered in a run-down hotel in the red-light district of Manila, where I was writing a piece on thirteenth-century assassins; there's another, my parents' friend who knew me when I was in the cradle.

What more could one ask of a companion? To be forever new and yet forever steady.

Even to bring them together, as when one introduces radically different friends at a party, could be treacherous: Emerson is a figure of light, singing of possibility, whereas Melville derives much of his dark charge from tearing away at all the hope that Emerson speaks for; Graham Greene is one of the last vestiges of a British Empire that Derek Walcott has been trying to urge into a new kind of miscegenated marriage. Just to have all of them together under the same roof at the same time, if they were walking and talking, would mean I would have to speak in many voices and many dialects all at once.

I first read *The Quiet American* maybe thirty years ago, and ever since then I have turned to it, my uncertain Bible, a gospel for those who can't be sure of a thing, every few months. Like any friend, it changes as I change, growing as I slowly come to know myself and the world a little better; and like any friend, it's always the same, really.

What more could one ask of a companion? To be forever new and yet forever steady. To be strange and familiar all at once, with enough change to quicken my mind, enough steadiness to give sanctuary to my heart. The books on my shelf never asked to come together, and they would not trust or want to listen to one another; but each is a piece of a stained-glass whole without which I wouldn't make sense to myself, or to the world outside.

Oliver Jeffers

⟶ *illustrator + artist* ⟵

I picked all of these books because I think you should *always* judge a book by its cover—or its spine, in this case. I collect books rather than hoard them. There's an editorial sense of selection that occurs. It's not all random. And I think this shelf is very aesthetically ordered. Some of the books are functional; I use them for illustrations. Like those orange encyclopedias. *Streets and Roads. The Illustrated Book of Wild Animals* is fabulous—I picked it up when I was in China. It's made up of a series of diagrams showing how to draw various wild animals. That last book on the end is *The Illustrated Book of Trees.* I just really like that color.

> *Books are everywhere in New York. People put them on the street when they're done reading them.*

The Downfall has one of the best covers I've ever seen. I love it. It's aesthetically gorgeous. And *The Homosexual Outlook*—I found that on the street and thought it was great. I have a younger brother who's gay, and I keep meaning to give it to him. But again, that yellow is so striking. The jacket of *The Ascent of Everest* is probably my favorite color. It's a great book, too. I like *Ivanhoe* because of its spine—it's beautiful—and that's basically it. A lot of my life has been about math and design, which is why I have *Basic Mathematics.* But I find that spine gorgeous as well. I keep it by my computer.

I tried not to do a shelf of favorite books, but *Catch-22* is one. The book runs true to so much of the art I make. Joseph Heller's ideas about the difference between logic and emotion, between what's cold and clinical and the spark of being alive—I think about that a lot with my work.

Books are everywhere in New York. People put them on the street when they're done reading them. My upstairs neighbor passed away recently, and I inherited her entire book collection. Which means my own collection just quadrupled. When I travel, I'll head to a flea market or an estate sale. People are always saying, "Never judge a book by its cover." But I think you have to ignore that advice, especially when you're working in the artistic side of publishing. People judge books by their covers every day.

Miranda July

writer + artist + filmmaker

A lot of times, especially when I'm writing a screenplay, I'll sit and flip through an art book. I don't own any scripts. For whatever reason, I never like to come straight at an idea. It's why I find a book like the Fischli & Weiss monograph very liberating—I'm looking at a different medium, and I can still see the common threads.

I'd put Lydia Davis in the same category. When I'm writing fiction, I'll flip to a page in her book and read a little bit. She's a reminder for me to be aware of what is happening to me right now. To ignore some larger literary striving that usually comes to no good. I don't write like her, but she makes me a better writer. I like to stay in touch with that book. And it's a nice book—I like the color of its cover.

Every time I look at that Moholy-Nagy book, I just laugh. It has all these pieces of paper stuck in it. It's not a book of beautiful pictures; it's just text. And that's not usually the kind of reader I am. But I got that book when I was twenty, and I love to see what I marked in it. What did I find so fascinating? Moholy-Nagy believes that we're all artists—it's just part of being a thinking, feeling human, he says—and that specializing in one medium is a trap.

People ask me all the time why I like to do so many different things, and even now, I hardly have an answer for them. I always say it's just very natural to me. But there must have been a point when I was working out that idea, and this book is evidence of that. I'd just dropped out of college. Everyone was asking me what I was doing with myself. And my answer wasn't very popular.

The North Star Man is a children's book—that's the same copy I had as a kid. It's about an old man whom these kids meet in a park. One day he takes them on a walk and shows them what's amazing about the Earth. Then he points to where he's from, way up in the sky, and when he leaves, he goes up with his umbrella. Kids aren't encouraged nowadays to talk to old men in parks and go on adventures with them, which is just too bad, in a way. I like the idea that a magical stranger—someone who doesn't even look like a magical stranger, who's just wearing a dusty old coat—could transform you and take you on a journey.

> *People ask me all the time why I like to do so many different things, and even now, I hardly have an answer for them. I always say it's just very natural to me.*

Maira Kalman

illustrator + writer

I was born in Israel and came to the United States when I was four. Hebrew was my first language, of course, but I learned English very quickly. We never bought books—that wasn't part of the vocabulary of what we bought—but my mother used to take me to the library, and we started at

I love the architecture of public libraries, the very large windows. Inside it's polished, it's quiet . . .

A and worked our way around. I love the architecture of public libraries, the very large windows. Inside it's polished, it's quiet; during the day, the sun is usually streaming through one room or another. And all the people are sitting there together, but they're all going to completely different places through the books they're reading.

I have always loved buying books, and I often say to myself, "I won't buy any books this week." Then, the next thing I know, I'm running over to twelve bookstores and frantically buying books as if I'm deprived. So I have thousands of books, and they're organized by subject and then alphabetically, pretty neatly, except when the system falls apart once in a while. My biggest collections are in photography, art, interior design, furniture and industrial design, illustration, the natural sciences, dictionaries, language books—that kind of thing.

The cell phone on this shelf is a beloved artifact from my son's late childhood, when he was in high school. This was when students were just beginning to have cell phones. I wasn't excited about it, so when he told me that all of his friends had them, I made him one out of cardboard. Fortunately, he had a good sense of humor, and he carried it with him to school. Maybe he was a little bit proud that he had such a nutty family.

Someone once asked me which arts I'm sad have been lost to our world, and I'm really sad that penmanship is gone, because the process of creating forms on the page—loving the words and loving the letters that make those words—is so satisfying. I like making letters. I would spend hours, when I was younger, writing out the alphabet over and over. Lately I've been writing *Mrs. Abraham Lincoln* in different letters, like somebody in sixth grade: *Mrs. Maira Lincoln.* I'm imagining that I was *the one* and that we have to send out invitations to our wedding party.

Zachary Kanin

—•→ *cartoonist* ←•—

It's hard to get away from a desert island scenario. You can't help but think of what you'd want to be left with. I put a lot of graphic novels on here, and a lot of story collections—all perfect desert island material. You're getting a lot per book with this shelf.

Daniel Clowes is great. I'm sure you've heard of *Ghost World*. *Like a Velvet Glove Cast in Iron* is a bizarre noir mystery without any real answers and with some very weird monsters. The dialogue in his books is different from anyone else's dialogue. And the characters he draws all have something *off* about them; even the beautiful ones will have a lazy eye or a missing chin.

The introduction to *A.L.I.E.E.E.N.* tells you it's a children's book for aliens that was found somewhere on Earth. The aliens speak a language of made-up hieroglyphics, and they're cute-looking—but they're all doing really disturbing things like dissecting one another and pooping. There's one alien who can't stop pooping—he's just filling up the entire world with poop and drowning everyone.

Tales Designed to Thrizzle is the Monty Python of comic books. One thing slips into the next. I saw Michael Kupperman give a reading once. He has whole panels where the entire time, the characters are just laughing. So there he was on stage, screaming, "Hah. Hah. Hah."

I draw about ten cartoons a week. For efficiency's sake, I know the basic settings I'm going to use—the furniture, the rooms, the drapes. Once you start shaking it up, though, more interesting things happen. I did a cartoon recently that showed two trees outside on a city street. You know how they're enclosed by those small fences to keep dogs from peeing on them? One tree says to the other, "If it wasn't for that tiny fence, I'd make a run for it." It's those little things that you don't even think about—like a miniature fence surrounding a tree—that can make the joke.

Sometimes I'll take a stack of computer paper and draw until strange things happen. I'll let my mind wander, and suddenly someone's leg will have gotten really long and turned into a bicycle, except it's a centaur bicycle. Then I try to resolve that. If I can, then maybe I'll have something. It's a lot of trial and error, a lot of sitting and thinking for hours.

In our fifth-grade yearbook, my classmates and I all had to write where we thought we'd be in 2010. I said I wanted to be married, and I wanted to be a cartoonist with a monkey bodyguard. Two out of three isn't bad. Or two and a half if you count my monkey butler.

Mary Karr

writer

As a child, I felt so bereft and abandoned by the world. I remember reading *The House at Pooh Corner,* and because it had a really sad ending, it actually made me feel less like a weirdo. It made me believe in the magic of literature. The same goes for my mother's edition of *Nine Stories.* Those were stories peopled by the dispossessed, the estranged. I loved them.

The Once and Future King let me read about a period of history that wasn't my own. It was a big leap. And it was so sad—all these good people hurting one another's feelings in profound ways. The betrayal that lay at the heart of it nearly broke me. But I loved its pageantry. It made me think of England as the origin of culture, just as Shakespeare did.

When I lived in England, I discovered Bishop and Larkin. For a long time, I wanted to be a poet. I wanted to be T. S. Eliot or Wallace Stevens. I didn't want to write autobiographically, I wanted to be cool and British and say things like "indeed." Alas, it was not to be. Instead, I found a totally different and brand-new way to humiliate myself.

To Kill a Mockingbird is about class as much as it is about race. As somebody who came from a class of people that was never written about or shown on television except in *The Beverly Hillbillies,* I found a sense of dignity in this book. And the closeness between Scout and Atticus was very much like what I felt with my own father, even though he was nothing like Atticus Finch. A lot of people have told me that I remind them of Scout. That would be perfect. That would mean I'd successfully stolen from Harper Lee, which has been one of my goals.

I found a totally different and brand-new way to humiliate myself.

If you want to write, don't err by setting the bar too low. Maybe you want to write like Emily Dickinson. Maybe you want to write like Nabokov. Just be willing, at the end of the day, to look at your work and say, "That's not as good as Nabokov, but boy, it's as good as I could make it today." Fall in love with books and with modes of being. I just spent a pile of money I can't afford on opera tickets to see Wagner's *Götterdämmerung.* Think of all the cocaine I could have bought with that eight hundred dollars! Yet here I am blowing it to go sit in a room with a bunch of stiffs next Tuesday night. I'm in love, I can't help it.

Thomas Keller

— chef + cookbook author —

A Treasury of Great Recipes by Mary and Vincent Price was my first cookbook. My mother gave it to me. I'm sure she

there are five or six books on this shelf that really will help you become a great chef.

bought it because it was the most ornate book on the cookbook shelf back then. It's leather-bound and gold-embossed, so I guess it made a big impression on her, and she thought it'd make a big impression on me, too. It's a wonderful story about the Prices' travels around the world, in Portugal, Spain, France, Italy, wherever. They write about their travels, describe the food they ate, and, of course, provide recipes for that food.

Roland Henin—who would later become my mentor—gave me Fernand Point's *Ma Gastronomie* in 1977. There really aren't any recipes in the book—it's mostly narrative—but its stories resonated with me because they were about a lifestyle. Fernand Point was a great figure in culinary history; he mentored and trained that next generation of chefs that I looked up to, people such as Paul Bocuse, Michel Guérard, and Alain Chapel. . . . I'm not

sure if these names mean anything to you, but perhaps you're getting a sense of the impact that Point himself had on the culinary world, and how the next generation after him affected that world on an international scale. And again, *The Great Chefs of France* is very similar. It cemented my desire to become a chef. There was this camaraderie, this interconnection among the chefs, this lifestyle, that really attracted me.

I think the most important part of this bookshelf, for someone who wants to become a chef, is understanding that there is a foundation to cooking, especially if you're going to do the type of food that I do. It begins in classic French cuisine and classic French technique, and in order to incorporate your own interpretation and your points of view into your cuisine, you need to have the basics. So there are five or six books on this shelf that really will help you become a great chef. But also sprinkled in are some wonderful books about life, books that are inspiring (Harry Truman's) and books about teamwork (John Wooden's). And there's some fun here, too. Because, at the end of the day? It's just food. That's all it is.

David Kelley

⏤•➤ *designer* ➤•⏤

I get my information and ideas from talking to people. That's who I am. Reading books is essential, but I'm more about personal contact than I am about reading. So these books represent people who were important to me.

Bob McKim was my mentor. I was lost in the woods as a bad engineer, I met him, and he made me realize what I was put on this Earth to do. When I was at Stanford, both he and James Adams taught me, more or less, a step-by-step approach enabling routine innovation. But they also gave me creative confidence. When you have that sort of self-assurance, you're more resistant to failure; you have different ideas, and you're willing to share them because you're not afraid of rejection. And in fact, you begin to think differently about everything in life, from building something to ordering Chinese food. Armed with that, you just *do* it. In my case, I started a company, I started designing things—I said, "Let's design a reading machine for blind people," and "Let's redesign the experience of checking into a hospital." Once you have creative confidence, you have everything.

An Incomplete Education is probably my favorite book. It talks a little bit about everything from British history to the theory of relativity. You might assume that because I'm an engineering professor, I must be narrowly focused, but I'm really not. My job, in some ways, is to build a stage and let others perform. I want to synthesize ideas. If I spend too much time in one area, I get uncomfortable. I try to be very broad and not very deep—we call it being T-shaped. A pianist, for example, is very deep and not very broad at the top of the T. Whereas I probably look more like a comb, with twenty-seven little teeth going down from the top.

I'm a car nut. I grew up in Barberton, Ohio, right next to Akron. Everybody there was a tire builder. The first thing I ever designed was a tandem bike—I welded two bikes together. Those Mailander books are the best car books you'll ever find. When you're restoring a car, it's so lovely to have photographs and anecdotes about it that can help you decide what's authentic and what's not. But I also believe, as a designer, that the car is the most important object of the twentieth century. It probably won't be the most important one of the twenty-first. The car is more than just a means of transportation. It has a lot of emotional meaning for us: it's about freedom, social mobility, self-expression. But maybe it's easier to say that because I'm just a kid from Ohio who likes cars.

Chuck Klosterman
—▸ writer ◂—

I was the seventh kid in my family. We lived in a relatively full house in North Dakota, and underneath the bed I inherited was a set of these very old encyclopedias. I remember that they were so old that Pluto had not yet been discovered when they were published. So that was what I read. I'd pick up the volume for *G,* say, and read all the entries that started with *G.*

I read *Season on the Brink* in high school. It's the only book that, immediately upon finishing it, I started again from the middle. I read it over and over. I was memorizing it. I really loved sports. I played sports. Maybe I thought I'd be a coach when I became an adult. But that was the first time I had ever read about sports the same way you might read about politics or culture. That book, in many ways, taught me how to be a sports writer.

Werner Herzog says that if you want to understand America, you have to read *The Warren Commission Report.* My first job was at a newspaper, and one of the things you're always told when you work at a paper is that journalism is important because it's the first draft of history. Well, *The Warren Report* is literally the first draft of what happened in the Kennedy assassination. It's a fascinating book to page through and read at random.

A Supposedly Fun Thing I'll Never Do Again is the best nonfiction writing I've ever seen in one spot. I know David Foster Wallace wanted to be thought of as a novelist, but I think he was more untouchable as a journalist. Before that book, I had come to the conclusion that a person could either be intellectual or be funny, but not both. Yet he'd often be both of those things in a single sentence.

Jerry Mander's *Four Arguments for the Elimination of Television* is a book that deals with the problems of accelerated culture and how the media change our relationship with reality. It's insane to realize that he published this in 1978. When I discovered this book—about five or six years ago—none of my writer friends had heard of it. I finally spoke to a friend in his fifties who's a librarian in Ohio, and he told me that back then, Mander's book was like *The Tipping Point.* It was *the* book to read if you were interested in culture. It occurred to me that if a nonfiction book experiences a massive spike in popularity, then the idea behind it becomes normative. And then the book itself completely disappears. Which made me wonder if the same thing could happen to me. My books, if they're truly successful, will become ideas that everyone accepts to be true, and the books themselves will disappear.

Lawrence Lessig

legal scholar + professor

When I was young, I was a Libertarian. I read everything I could find by Ayn Rand. Her characters are strong-willed people with such conviction in their conception of what is right. They defend it and fight for it. That sort of romantic idealism and integrity can of course seem naive and ridiculous to an adult, but as a kid, I found those qualities incredibly attractive.

Edith Wharton suited a later, almost anti-Libertarian stage in my thinking. I read her in the middle of law school. She is obsessed with the way in which social context defines or blocks the souls inside it. I became similarly fixated on how context constructs us. Reading Wharton taught me the practice of stepping inside a location and looking not at what was happening in the foreground but rather at what was going on in the background. Virginia Woolf was then an escape from Wharton, allowing for the possibility that a person might stride out into the day, as in the first scene of *Mrs. Dalloway,* and build an idea of herself or himself against or apart from a constricting social background.

I became a lawyer because I had an uncle who was counsel to the House Judiciary Committee during the Watergate hearings. After the committee approved the article to impeach Nixon, my uncle took me for a walk and explained to me that the law was a domain in which power was exercised through reason, as opposed to the market, where wealth is power, or the military, where force is power. There was something very compelling for me in the notion of using this tool to rebuild parts of our society that were unjust or incomplete.

I've always been interested in science fiction and technology. *Snow Crash* was my point of entry into the work I eventually did with the law of cyberspace. It was the cue I needed to realize how thoroughly we might be molded, regardless of our wishes, by our environment—here a technical environment, and not, as in Wharton, a normative one.

I think of this bookshelf as a philosophy course in how to look at the world. Some ideas are smaller than others, such as copyright. That's a particular struggle or insight. But others are more general—ways to think about how culture, and we its inhabitants, are constructed. These books would teach the things I believe quite effectively and powerfully.

Jonathan Lethem
⟶ writer ⟵

I have to admit that I picked this group of books partly in response to seeing the paintings of other people's shelves, which had so many contemporary titles in them. My relationship to my own book collection tends to be really eccentric. It's a very specific, decrepit attraction: I like old books.

The Shipwrecked is a marvelous peculiarity. If you know Graham Greene at all well, it must seem like a stumper. This was an early novel of his called *England Made Me,* which, when the book was first published in the United States, his American publisher didn't think was a promotable title. So it was renamed for the American market. Now, this is not the sort of thing you would think would happen to a writer of the stature of Graham Greene, but back then he wasn't yet the giant figure of years to come, who would have been able to say, "Use my original title or to hell with you!"

each of these books is a vast experience unto itself, while also being both self-contained and superbly useless.

As a book collector, I love these elements of literary history that lie buried and waiting to be discovered in old editions. There is no other reason to know that one of Graham Greene's books was once called *The Shipwrecked* unless you happened across that strange purple hardcover. I treasure stuff like that.

Walking Small was the first novel I ever read by a writer I knew personally. L. J. Davis lived a couple of blocks away from me on Dean Street in Brooklyn. I was probably fourteen, maybe fifteen when I met him. Suddenly I had this opportunity to put together a human being—a very eccentric and marvelous character living down the street—with a narrative novelist's voice. I found it totally compelling. To me, it was a glimpse of something hallowed to go to L.J.'s house and see his typewriter and realize he had written that book while sitting right there.

The thing about this bookshelf is that each of these books is a vast experience unto itself, while also being both self-contained and superbly useless. Reading any one of them doesn't get you anywhere particularly meaningful; you haven't arrived or graduated; you've just gone and done something that passed the time. It's like taking a long walk with a friend who's got a lot to say. There's no cumulative purpose to it—it's just an excellent way to waste your life.

Yiyun Li

writer

I love William Trevor. He is the only living author whom I read constantly. My whole career is indebted to his writing. There was a period of time when I would finish a story and send it to him. I imagined that my stories were having a conversation with his. Even though I write about different places and different people, I think our stories are speaking to one another.

I was at Iowa as an MFA student, and I remember reading a very odd story by Trevor in _The New Yorker_. It was about a boarding school, and it was called "Traditions." I had to know more, so I checked _After Rain_ out of the library. I remember reading it in the lobby of the Iowa Memorial Union. I couldn't move. That was the beginning of my falling in love with his stories.

I came to Iowa from China. I entered as a scientist and left as a writer. I'll tell you what happened to me: I probably just went mad. That's the only explanation. I was a very good scientist, but I wasn't very dedicated. I wanted to do something else. I had never written fiction, and I had never written in English. The idea of doing both of those things was incredibly appealing to me. My children recently informed me that my English is really bad. But I believe that on a daily basis, no matter the language, you have to struggle to put thought into words.

I had this idea that I was undereducated when it came to the liberal arts. During my second year at Iowa, I began to study Latin with a tutor. She would meet me once a week in a room at the public library. I decided that if I really wanted to learn the language, I should start by reading children's books. So I checked out _Winnie ille Pu_ from the library. My tutor asked me if I had ever heard of the book before. I hadn't, of course. She told me to get the English version.

To me, poetry is the thing that is the most difficult to master when you write in a second language. Writing prose is one thing, but writing poetry is something else. I put Elizabeth Bishop on my shelf because I love her poems. I used to read one poem of hers a day. I actually think that's a much harder goal to maintain than, say, reading fifty-two pages of a novel a day. It would take me an hour to finish a poem—and her poems aren't very long. I had to read her word by word. Again and again.

> _I believe that on a daily basis, no matter the language, you have to struggle to put thought into words._

Pamela Love

jewelry designer

I wanted to be a painter or an installation artist when I was younger. I was really interested in Joseph Cornell. I loved his stuff. Most of my house turned into a Joseph Cornell box.

Francesco Clemente is on my shelf because I assisted him for five years; he was my mentor. He really inspired my aesthetic and sensibilities; he solidified the idea that what I found interesting was important, that it could be art. It was so incredible to be in that world. I had come from an office job, which I hated, and to go from that to working with my hands around this extremely creative person taught me confidence. He feels very strongly about his ideas and moves forward without hesitation. That is something I learned from him.

For me, making jewelry is about crafting a story, creating a world—the objects I make are artifacts from that world.

Jewelry was just a hobby for me at first. I was making it on the side, and I was lucky that people were interested in buying what I was producing. So it slowly turned into a business, but I had to teach myself everything about it. Every season is different. When I'm inspired by something, I want to put myself in it and be entirely surrounded by it. I'll travel, I'll read, I'll look at pictures, everything. From there, I'll start sketching and carving, which makes it easier to imagine. For me, making jewelry is about crafting a story, creating a world—the objects I make are artifacts from that world.

I am so inspired by the way Georgia O'Keeffe lived, which is why I have her portrait book on here. I love her work, but even more than that, I love her life—how she isolated herself from the world, how she lived in the desert, the imagery of skulls and nature that she surrounded herself with. I dressed up as her for Halloween last year. There's this photo of her walking in the New Mexico desert: she's in this weird long dress with a head wrap, wearing a pair of Keds and dragging a giant deer skull around. So I put on a weird long dress and Keds, I spray-painted my hair gray, and I dragged around a skull all night—it was great, even though nobody knew who I was supposed to be.

Larissa MacFarquhar
⤜• *writer* •⤞

When I graduated from college, I thought I wanted to work in human rights, but it turned out I couldn't get a job—even an entry-level one—without a law degree, so I ended up, somewhat randomly, working at the *Paris Review* as an intern, and from there I decided that I wanted to be a journalist. I joined *The New Yorker* in 1998 and have been there ever since.

> *People are always saying that it's harder to write simply and clearly than to write in a complex manner, but that's nonsense.*

I am always pushing Kenneth Tynan on people. He's a British writer who wrote for *The New Yorker* in the sixties, near the end of his career, but I've found that most people in this country haven't heard of him. When he was young, his writing was fantastically baroque—each noun would have seventeen adjectives, and each verb had an adverb, and everything was ornamented to the last degree. It's terrific stuff. People are always saying that it's harder to write simply and clearly than to write in a complex manner, but that's nonsense. Simple language is usually the easiest to write: most of us just don't have the energy to make every sentence a work of art.

Most sentences are merely functional, they get you from A to B, and that's okay, up to a point. But I love Kenneth Tynan because every one of his sentences is wrought like a Fabergé egg. Every image is unexpected. It's exhilarating, and it raises my standards. Reading him, I remember that it's not enough to say that someone has brown hair. Because what does that tell you? Nothing.

What Maisie Knew tells the story of a marriage through the eyes of a young child. She knows that something not quite right is going on with her family, and she's trying to figure out what it is with the little she can see and deduce. It's a kind of slow-motion detective story. I think that writing fiction from the perspective of a child is generally a bad idea, but James does it so beautifully, so deftly, that he manages to make the thoughts convincingly those of a child without resorting to any of *The Sound and the Fury*'s heavy machinery: the language is his, it isn't childish.

One of the reasons this book has stuck in my head all these years is that I'm trying to do something similar when I write a profile: ideally I want the piece to seem, in some sense, as though it were coming from the person I'm writing about, rather than from me, even though the writing is obviously mine.

John Maeda

graphic designer + computer scientist

I found Paul Rand's book by accident. I was an undergraduate at MIT when I stumbled across it in the library. It introduced me to the world of graphic design. I had been informally designing as a hobby on my computer, but I had no idea that design existed as its own field. And it was incredibly humbling to see what Paul Rand was doing, to realize how far I had to go. His work is really thoughtful, but it's also playful and sad, gorgeous and warm, all at the same time. That book began my buying spree focused on expensive design books. It was a bad habit. But now I own only about forty books, because when I first got to RISD, I donated my collection to the library. These are basically what I have left.

My first computer was an Apple II. I must have been twelve or thirteen when I got it. It didn't do anything at all. There was no software, no Internet, no connectivity; you had to program it yourself. That C book was my first computer-programming book. It's so thin! It was a lot easier back then. Now you have to buy a ten-volume series; I couldn't learn it if I tried. You turn on the computer, and it wants to know everything about you; it's a whole different world. But what's missing is the making part. We used to *make* before. Now we spend so much time *consuming*.

I'm a person who needs to see something before I can understand it. I've designed my books myself. Every command-shift 3, every CMYK separation, every crop. That's how I am, how I make sense of things. But I put *Artful Sentences* by Virginia Tufte on my shelf because it's a beautiful book about writing. She's the mother of Edward Tufte, the famous visualization guru. Writing is what makes a difference in the end. Visuals help, but you have to have good content.

Atul Gawande's *Better* presents a theory about self-improvement. You can't expect a miracle overnight, he says; you won't get twice as good at something in just an hour. It's about becoming 1 percent better every year by finding the few things you can change within your process. He applies the notion to his own work as a surgeon: if doctors and nurses washed their hands more often, he points out, it would significantly lower the number of patients who become sick while in the hospital. That's what I aspire to do: I want to do 1 percent better, or even just 0.1 percent better. On some days, that's the best you can strive for.

> We used to make before. Now we spend so much time consuming.

Stephin Merritt

musician

I never wanted to be a musician. I still don't. It's what I've fallen into, really. I wanted to be a filmmaker. I went to film school. Before that, I wanted to be a planetarium artist. You know those artists who work in planetaria? I assumed those people were actually artists. I thought it was a guild. But apparently it doesn't work that way.

Berlin Alexanderplatz is *the* book that I have still not read page 1 of even after trying to make myself read it for twenty years. I want to read it before I see the movie. I've had the DVD since the day it came out, maybe ten years ago. It's from the Criterion Collection. I have everything by Fassbinder, everything you can get on DVD by Fassbinder that's playable in America, so it's absurd that I haven't seen it. In the time it's taken me not to read *Alexanderplatz*, I have read five Fassbinder biographies. I have a burning desire to read it. I have no idea why I haven't done it.

> *I have a burning desire to read it. I have no idea why I haven't.*

In a sense, Fassbinder made me want to be a filmmaker. But I was terrible at it. No talent whatsoever. You need to be able to tell stories, and you need to care whether or not the camera is in focus. I actually quite admire the early Warhol films, in which Warhol can't tell a story and doesn't care whether the camera is in focus. It may explain my attraction to Fassbinder as well. For them, it was about working with a fascinating company of actors. So I guess what I really wanted to do as a filmmaker was put together the equivalent of a band. And if I could, I would have had a group of people to film whom I could order around. And torture. It's a step down from wanting to be a planetarium artist. Now I just keep my megalomania in check by having four bands.

I used to read *Ethan Frome* every year on my birthday. It's ninety-nine pages long and really easy to read in one day. It seems very different to me every time I read it. It was something I did for about ten years before I finally decided that it was the wrong book to read on my birthday: it's as tragic as they come. I don't remember how I got into doing that in the first place; no doubt I was in my early twenties and feeling terribly, terribly sorry for myself. Now I've learned that when I feel sorry for myself, I can just write an album about it instead.

Stephenie Meyer

writer

I was the reader. That was my identity in my family: I was that girl who was always in a corner reading; I read my whole life away. I skipped children's books. My dad would read to us at night, and I first began to read on my own by reading ahead in those books. I was seven when I read *Little Women* for the first time, and it became nearly as real to me as the rest of my life.

I always identified with Jo; I was the tomboy. My big sister was Meg, the pretty one, the sweet one. We didn't have a Beth, but my younger sister was definitely Amy, the frivolous one who liked nice things. I was like Jo in every way except for her passion for writing; I was perfectly content just to read. It wasn't until much later, after I had published three books, that I went back to *Little Women* and realized that I had become even more like Jo. Now I was a writer, too.

Of all the heroines I was invested in throughout my childhood, Jane Eyre was the one I most identified with, despite my having a happy and supportive family. I liked heroines who weren't perfectly beautiful. I liked that everyone wasn't swept away and captivated by her. Jane Eyre has this huge stubborn streak, which I have, too. I have my ideals, and I really don't diverge from them—it's

probably off-putting to a lot of people. Jane is like that, too; she sticks to things even when she's uncomfortable and unhappy and making other people feel the same way. Of course, she's pushed to deeper extremes than I've ever been forced to go to, but I always felt we would see eye to eye.

When I think about the books that were formative to me as a writer, I can see how much I was influenced by *Anne of Green Gables*. When the series starts, Anne is a young girl, and we follow her as she becomes a teenager, an adult, a mother, and finally almost a grandmother. It's so rare that we get to grow up with a character. When I was first imagining my novels, I skipped from *Twilight* to *Breaking Dawn* because I was eager to see Bella as an adult. My editor encouraged me to slow down and show more of her in high school. I don't enjoy a character as much when he or she stays the same age. I want to see what comes next.

These books contain threads of what I like to write about: the way people interact, how we relate to one another when life is both beautiful and horrible. But these books are greater than anything I could ever aspire to create. I'll never love what I've done as much as I love what these authors have done. However, for me, just getting to create is its own reward.

Marilyn Minter

artist

I read Andy Warhol before I even moved to New York; I wanted to know how a great artist thought. I grew up in the Deep South, and I spent my whole life just trying to get here. There wasn't even a minute when I thought I'd do something else. As a kid, I taught myself how to draw by copying the illustrations from Andersen's *Fairy Tales.*

To make art in extreme poverty, to have a vision and have support but not have any material resources—there's an incredible purity in that experience for an artist.

I wasn't accomplished; I just didn't have choices. It was the only thing I could do.

I'm fascinated by biographies of artists. I read them all the time. I have a huge stack of biographies. The de Kooning is so interesting: he did these pastel Picassos up until he was forty, and then he made this giant leap into abstraction; it wasn't until pretty late in his life that his career took off. To make art in extreme poverty, to have a vision and have support but not have any material resources—there's an incredible purity in that experience for an artist.

The biography of Diane Arbus is one of the better ones. I think there is a lot of tenderness in her work; she was never trying to be salacious with her freaks, she was just making a picture of what was in front of her.

I met Arbus for about a minute. Here's what happened: I was an undergraduate at the University of Florida. The head of the photography department was this really romantic guy—he was technically a genius, but his content was corny as hell, and Diane Arbus hated all the graduate work she had seen. So the department head told me to show her my proof sheets of these pictures I had taken of my drug-addict mother. And Diane Arbus really liked them. I didn't think they were that extraordinary; I didn't know how weird my mother looked to other people. My brothers and I still look at those pictures and don't see what everybody else sees. I had no idea who Arbus was then; it was only after she killed herself, two years later, that I really looked at her work.

Thurston Moore

~ *musician* ~

Patti Smith's *Seventh Heaven* was a very significant book for me. I remember going to the Gotham Book Mart in 1977 because I'd heard that was where William Burroughs hung out, and while I was there I bought a copy of *Seventh Heaven*. I loved the aesthetic of that stark black-and-white cover image; it was very urban at a time when most rock music was romanticizing this rural hippie look. Patti's pieces were really ecstatic and sexual, which meant something to a seventeen-year-old boy looking to identify with art.

I bought a lot of books by Telegraph Press after that; they were all the same trim size, with the same typewriter fonts and the same black-and-white images on the front. And I discovered all those New York poets, people like Gerard Malanga and Ted Berrigan. I identify that book as my entry point into small-press poetry, even though I didn't know what small-press poetry was at the time.

I display *Where I Hang My Hat* face out because the cover is by Joe Brainard, another New York poet whom I've always loved. He made dust-jacket illustrations for a number of small-press poetry books in the sixties and seventies—they're very minimal and plain, but sweet and evocative at the same time.

I get asked a lot about the difference between song-writing and poetry. I think the poetic voice is much more of a solitary endeavor. Poetry itself can be collaborative, but the actual *life* of a poet is a solitary exercise of expressing emotional ideas on the page. With a band, you want it to be a unified democracy; you want to have a voice that's shared—unless you're a singer-songwriter who dictates everything to the other musicians, which is definitely the case for some. But I think the most interesting bands are the ones that have a communal tongue, as it were.

I've never actually read *The Cosmological Eye*. I'm a little on the fence about Henry Miller because of the misogyny of his books. I know he's a product of his time, and I do appreciate *Tropic of Cancer:* it opened me up to the idea of spontaneous prose writing, and Miller's relentless obsession with the idea of an intensified relationship is fascinating. But I remember buying *The Cosmological Eye* because I was attracted to the cover, which features this beautiful black-and-white eyeball. I will read it some day.

Most of the books that I have in my library are unread. A lot of them are almost like pieces of art, sort of tactile—I pick them up, touch them and look at them, and get vibrations from them. The fact that I can eventually read them and glean their content is an added bonus.

Nico Muhly
composer

I love to read on my iPad because I travel so much. I used to have a big ol' apartment, but I've moved to a smaller place, and now all of my books are stored in my mother's house in Vermont. Now I have just two shelves for books—mostly gifts, reference books, and music stuff that I need on a daily basis. People still give me hardcover books, which is insane. I was given this book of Matisse prints that is literally larger than any other object in my apartment. It's a coffee-table book, but what kind of coffee table does this person think I have?

> *It's a coffee-table book, but what coffee table do they think I have?*

There was something a little strange to me about curating a bookshelf; it's not how my mind works. I'd rather you saw what I'm reading at this particular time. Take it or leave it. I guess there would be a way to choose an ideal bookshelf so it was just novels by homosexual writers of a certain era or all religious texts or all biographies of serial killers. But surely the point is to be able to read about Kim Jong Il, then two seconds later consult a book about Rose West, and then two seconds later learn how to fold shrimp paste into a pancake. Everything should constantly be in play.

This is a capricious moment for me. I'm not actually using any of these books for anything I'm writing. Well, actually the Wycliffe New Testament, which is this crazy translation, is turning up in a song. But these are subjects that I'm casually interested in, to no particular end. I'm not going to write the Rosemary West oratorio for fifteen violas—though maybe that wouldn't be a bad idea.

I think a lot of people have this idea of the composer as a hero, as some brilliant, flawed genius living in a hut in the woods. But the composers whom I identify with most were state employees. They usually worked for the church or the government, which at the time were basically the same thing: William Byrd, Orlando Gibbons, Thomas Weelkes, Thomas Tallis. They were on the clock. They weren't lying by some stream bank and communing with nature. It was more like, the choir was coming in at four-thirty to sing every song that had been sung every night in that very same location since the Reformation; there was no room for romanticizing the process because they had to get something on the music stands. And the music they wrote under such constraints, by the way, is some of the most beautiful and the most ravishing music you'll ever hear.

Kate & Laura Mulleavy

fashion designers

LAURA: We work as one person; all of our differences eventually lead to one viewpoint.

KATE: We've always created together. We were inseparable as children. Our minds think as one and the same. We wanted to choose books that meant something to us when we were growing up. Or books that taught us to visualize and imagine worlds that we were not living in, spaces we weren't a part of.

LAURA: We grew up in a quiet town outside of Santa Cruz. Our father was a botanist who studied myxomycetes, or slime molds. He was obsessed with microscopic things. One of his hobbies was flying small planes, which we always thought he did in order to experience the world from a distance, so that everything became tiny. Our mother was an artist. She was constantly exploring different media: painting, weaving, mosaics, sculpture. In many ways, it was a very fantastical childhood. We were always in the forest. We put *John Muir in Yosemite* on our shelf because Muir's writings and observations helped save places such as Yosemite and Sequoia National Park, some of the most magnificent natural wonders in the United States.

KATE: I think reading is an escape. It allows you to imagine whole worlds. It's incredible that we learn to be who we are through text. We become compassionate beings because we are taught to live in the lives of others. *Frankenstein*—in both the Mary Shelley and the Boris Karloff incarnations—inspired our fall 2009 collection. Which is why we included Shelley's novel here.

LAURA: When you drive north on the Pasadena Freeway, you pass a cluster of old Victorian homes. One day we noticed that a piece of insulation had fallen off of one of those houses, and that got us to thinking about the architectural interventions of the artist Gordon Matta-Clark. He used to cut away whole sections of a building, its floors, ceilings, walls. We began to reexamine Victorian homes as sites of assembly. In some ways, we thought, they were pieced together just like Frankenstein's monster. And we realized that the world we wanted to create was one of a deconstructed site, one that was both archaic and futuristic, with layers upon layers of texture: piles of rock, granite, marble, and ore. We wanted to explore the processes of building, ruin, and preservation.

The starting point can happen at any moment. All storytellers, no matter what medium they're working in, are compelled to consider what others may be overlooking. It's simply a matter of opening your eyes.

Mira Nair

— *filmmaker* —

I grew up in a small town in East India, and I went to an Irish-Catholic convent school. There was a nun, the most legendary nun—Sister Joseph Catherine—who taught *only* literature. My first class with her was on onomatopoeia, and she made me fall slam-bang in love with words and with Shakespeare and Blake and Keats. In postcolonial India, you think in English, the goddamned language of the colonizers. Thanks to this nun, it was English that first captivated me. The extraordinary poetry of Urdu and Hindu came to me much later.

A room is not a room without books. I love the tactile quality of reaching for a book and being transported to somewhere else for an hour or even a second. In 1975, twenty-one books came to me in New Delhi in a package from England. I was fifteen, and I had ordered every book that Dylan Thomas ever published. He taught me a love of words, of the circus of wrestling with them, of voluptuous vocabulary. I had never read writing like his. It was books and what they did to the imagination that made me finally cross the oceans and be who I am.

> A room is not a room without books.

There is one book on this shelf that led me to my husband, Mahmood Mamdani: *From Citizen to Refugee,* which he wrote in 1973. It was 1988, and I was making a film about the expulsion of Asians from Uganda—*Mississippi Masala.* When I read the book, I felt like I knew this man. It was an incredibly personal and yet political account of being expelled as a Ugandan Asian, and I wanted to talk to him. My assistant at the time managed to track him down. He was a professor at the University of Kampala, and he was one of the many people I was due to meet with when I went there for research. It was love at first sight. And here we are now, over twenty years later.

Christoph Niemann

—•» *illustrator* «•—

Jenö Barcsay's *Anatomie für Künstler* is the best anatomy book I've ever seen. I got it for Christmas when I was fourteen, and I remember spending months and months with it, looking at the hands, the bodies, everything. Even then, my fascination with the human body was about being able to draw proper faces and muscles. Learning how they functioned on a biological scale made all the difference.

The Master and Margarita and Flann O'Brien were both recommended to me by my art academy teacher Heinz Edelmann. He got me reading more than anybody else. Edelmann did a lot of amazing poster art and book covers in the sixties and seventies—he made the art for *Yellow Submarine.* I loved O'Brien for his humor. And the way he describes the Irish: they're so miserable that when it stops raining, they have to beat each other up.

I loved *The Corrections,* and I liked *Freedom* even more. But the books to which I feel a very special connection are the ones I discovered by myself. With Jonathan Franzen, it was impossible not to know that he had a new novel out. But in the case of *I Served the King of England,* I remember buying it in a bookshop just because I liked the cover. I thought it was my very own little gem, even though I eventually found out that Hrabel is quite well known. The

same was true for me with Raymond Pettibon, who is incredibly famous. But I still recall being in Printed Matter in SoHo in the midnineties and seeing a book of his there. To this day, I feel like he's mine.

I think the most successful illustrations are the those that build on some other reference. You can't completely reinvent something. It's like headlines, where often the funniest ones are based on puns. When I'm making a *New Yorker* cover, that's the best way to approach it: I mentally browse through my list of visual clichés and try to mess with them, get to the left or the right of the meaning. I like *The New Yorker* because it's the only magazine that lets the image do all the work. It's like the Olympics for illustrators.

For me, David Foster Wallace is almost painful to read. It's like he's mumbling. You think he's just writing down every single idea that comes into his head, but then when you reach the end, you realize that every sentence has been perfectly composed. I wish I could find something in his work that I could put to use in my own. But it's like watching Lionel Messi play soccer: all I can do is sit there and enjoy it with my mouth hanging open. The difference between his brilliance and my capabilities is just too big.

Sigrid Nunez
— writer —

The Grimm Brothers' *Household Tales* and Edith Hamilton's *Mythology* were my favorite childhood reading. From them I learned, among other things, the power and magic of storytelling. They cast a spell on me—I could not stop reading them over and over—and inspired my first attempts at writing stories and poetry.

J. M. Coetzee is one of my literary heroes. I've read most of his work and admire equally his fiction and nonfiction. *Boyhood: Scenes from Provincial Life* is a memoir, though it's written in the third person. Like most of his books, it's quite short, and the style is austere. To me, the restraint and asceticism of Coetzee's writing make so much other writing, however fine it may be, seem undisciplined by comparison. I'm also fascinated by the way he blurs the line between novel and autobiography. The term he uses for a book like *Boyhood* is "*autre*-biography."

Several of the other books I've chosen are also hybrids. The work of Lydia Davis, another literary hero of mine, has been described as a mix of fiction, poetry, philosophical essay, and lyric essay. (I just call it genius.) *The Meadow,* James Galvin's stunningly beautiful history of a piece of land that lies on the border between two Western states, is a book that itself lies on the border between fiction and

nonfiction. Michael Herr's *Dispatches,* based on his experiences as a war correspondent in Vietnam, is anything but fiction, alas. But it's also something beyond ordinary journalism: a thrilling collage that's part reportage, part personal journal, part travel writing, and part stream-of-consciousness storytelling. Read it and reel.

The poet Rilke's only novel, *The Notebooks of Malte Laurids Brigge,* is one of the most original books in modern literature. It tells the story of a young Danish aristocrat and poet living in Paris, but so much of Rilke's own life and thought bleeds into Malte's that it often reads like autobiography. I read it for the first time in college on the recommendation of my writing teacher, Elizabeth Hardwick, who considered the book essential. It was a major influence on her novel *Sleepless Nights,* another work that could be described as part fiction, part essay, part autobiography.

I remember once telling Hardwick what a hard time I was having trying to write what would turn out to be the first part of my first book: the story of my immigrant parents and their troubled marriage. Hardwick replied that it was a matter of tone: "If you find the right tone," she said, "you can write about anything." I've never forgotten that remark, and of course it's absolutely true.

James Patterson
—•→ writer ←•—

Gabriel García Márquez's *One Hundred Years of Solitude* floored me as a younger reader. I think it drove me into writing thrillers, because I realized I couldn't do anything at his level. So I decided to try something that I might be capable of doing well. I had read a few thrillers and liked them, and thought I might be able to write in that genre.

The first time I was told that a book of mine had hit the *New York Times* bestseller list, I didn't believe it. I went to a Barnes & Noble near my apartment. While I'm there, this woman picks up my book. Now, I think a lot of writers do this. If we see somebody pick up our book in a store, we're going to watch them, you know? So I watch this lady, and she reads the flap, then she opens up the book and reads a few pages. I'm watching her: if she buys the book, it'll make my week; if she sets it down again, it'll break my heart. She puts it under her arm and makes her way toward the front of the store, and I'm flying—This is the greatest thing! I think to myself; supposedly I'm on the *Times* bestseller list, the stack of copies in the store is getting low—and then I see her stuff my book into her handbag and walk out. She stole it! I couldn't believe it. All I could think about was whether or not it would count as a sale.

Readers know that if they pick up one of my books, the story is really going to zip along.

Stephen King has been busting my chops for years, but I'll put one of his books on my shelf. I don't know if I like him, but I like *Different Seasons* a lot. He's a bit like the bully in your high school. He once wrote something like "James Patterson is not cool and has never been cool." But you know what? I'm actually cool. My teenage son thinks I'm pretty cool, and kids don't like anybody. So come on, Uncle Stevie, let's have a coffee. Then you can go out and trash me.

I don't see myself as a brand, but I think I am in touch with what a lot of people want. Readers know that if they pick up one of my books, the story is really going to zip along. They're going to have strong feelings one way or the other about the characters. I think my readers know what they're going to get in my books. For better or worse, I get right into the story. It's like that rule of real estate, "Location, location, location," except for me it's "Story, story, story." I think it'd be disastrous if everyone wrote the way I do. But I think it's good that somebody does.

Nancy Pearl
—⤜ librarian ⤛—

I knew I wanted to be a librarian when I was ten years old. As a child growing up in Detroit, I felt as though I lived in the Parkman Branch Library, where the children's librarians took me under their wing and opened up the world of books and reading to me. It was the most welcoming place. I went there every day after school. On Saturdays, I would pack a lunch, ride my bike or walk, and be there when the library opened at 9:00 a.m., leaving only at 5:30 p.m., when it closed. I reasoned that if I wanted to do some good in the world—I was that kind of child, the sort who thought about things like that at the age of ten— what could I do that would be better than helping other children the way those librarians helped me?

These are my favorite books. Some are out of print, and some are going to be reissued in the Book Lust Rediscoveries series. I really believe that there are so many good books out there, but it's often hard to find them. Too many are obscured by the current stuff that's being widely publicized. I am always interested in finding hidden gems. My all-time favorite book is Merle Miller's *A Gay and Melancholy Sound*—I have never forgotten how I found it

It's the kind of book you want to hug. All of these books are.

and where I was. I was wandering through the library in Annapolis, Maryland, and happened to see the title. It was a nice, thick book. I picked it up and fell in love with it.

I think Neal Stephenson's *Cryptonomicon* has everything you could need in a science-fiction book: history, code breaking, and what I like to call elastic realism. Nora Johnson's *A Step beyond Innocence* is about a young woman who goes off to college and learns about life and love. I first read that book a long, long time ago, but I can still remember some of the scenes in it so vividly. I have only a very old library copy that I found after it had been discarded. It's the kind of book you want to hug. All of these books are. I loved reading every one of them.

I believe in libraries. Everyone who enters the library is equal. You have a right to be there. You don't have to pay. You don't have to be of a certain ethnicity. You don't have to belong to a certain religion. It's a place where information and the love of reading are both valued. And librarians are there to help the members of the public find what they need to live and to make their lives better.

Francine Prose
writer

I'll tell you something: when I was first asked to put together an "ideal bookshelf," I couldn't do the choosing. This is about problems I have; this is why there are a gazillion bookshelves in my house. I knew that it would take me six months to make the selection. So instead I decided to use a bookshelf that already existed. My husband and I found the Max and monster dolls in New Orleans. My granddaughter was obsessed with *Where the Wild Things Are.*

Reading Chekhov shares a quality with looking at certain kinds of great art: both activities feel like a religious experience.

I also got her this tea set on eBay; it's very much like the one I remember having myself as a little girl. My study is where my granddaughter and I hang out. One day, she thought Max and monster should have tea. So now we have tea. We play. The dolls have complete lives. They wear jewelry. They go to restaurants and movies. They like Mexican food. They're like five-year-old New Yorkers. And then they go back up with the Chekhov books.

Chekhov saved my sanity, or what was left of my sanity. It was 1986, the winter when the *Challenger* blew up, and I was commuting from the country to teach at Sarah Lawrence. It was a messy time, and all I read was Chekhov. When I taught, I would tell my students what they couldn't do with fiction. And then, later that same day, I would read something by Chekhov in which he did exactly what I had just told my students not to do. It was an education for me.

I only wish he influenced my own writing. Reading Chekhov shares a quality with looking at certain kinds of great art: both activities feel like a religious experience. They're "uplifting." Sometimes I wonder if there are any differences between short-story writers and novelists. One difference might be that short-story writers can allow themselves to pursue perfection. They never have to deal with baggy writing, with three hundred useless pages. They can polish and polish. But then I remember that Chekhov wrote six hundred stories. And that he died at the young age of forty-four. David Gates asked this about Charles Dickens, but you could ask it about Chekhov, too: "Was he a Martian?" He was not from this planet.

Ishmael Reed

writer + cartoonist + jazz musician

I wrote my name in kindergarten, and I ran all the way home. Since then, I've always been fascinated by writing. I use all different forms of storytelling—I think that's why I've survived. I have the ability to talk back, to fight back, in a number of forms: songs, novels, plays, essays, poetry, etc. Reading other black male writers provided me with a handbook on how to survive in a racist country where black men are popularized by others as brutes and buffoons.

Richard Wright's *Black Boy* is one of those manuals for survival if you're a black man. It tells you what to look for, how to pay attention to the dog whistles. Take this election coming up in 2012—it's like a chorale of dog whistles. The Republicans are subtly talking about race, bringing up black bucks and welfare queens. But we listen. We know. We remember. *Black Boy* covers a lot of that territory. Richard Wright's daughter, Julia Wright, wasn't allowed as a child to use the restroom in Bloomingdale's. When I was a kid, we were on Lookout Mountain in Chattanooga, and I drank from a water fountain. My mother told me I couldn't drink from it, and I didn't understand. Countee Cullen, one of the great poets of the 1920s Harlem Renaissance, wrote a poem entitled

"Incident" about when he was a child and someone first called him by the n-word: *I saw the whole of Baltimore / From May until December; / Of all the things that happened there / That's all that I remember. /* Every one of us has had, or will have, what I call our own Baltimore moment. We all remember our first encounter with racism. I also remember being taken to Kansas City at some point in the early forties, at a time when there was a hit song playing on the radio called "Don't Sit under the Apple Tree (with Anyone Else but Me)." We were on a segregated train, and I wandered into the white section. I started singing that song. I was maybe three or four. My mother came to get me, but everybody in the white car told her I could stay. They all loved me. As long as I entertained them, they accepted me. I always say, we didn't need the theater to be absurd, because we had the South. The South was our theater of the absurd.

I consider myself a writer in exile. I get my books published in Canada now, by a small press. When black writers in the nineteenth century couldn't get published in America, they went to Canada. I even wrote a novel called *Flight to Canada,* but I never thought I'd be the one taking the flight! Given what I know, I find it deliciously ironic.

Alex Ross

writer

In high school, I was overwhelmed by Mahler. I have hundreds of scores—this is a miniature score of his Ninth Symphony that I bought fairly early on. Scores are books, too, and they can be quite beautiful to look at: patterns often jump out at you when you experience music as a visual phenomenon. I've always found it puzzling that so many see classical music as a reserved or overly intellectual genre, because that's never been my experience.

Mahler's is some of the most unreservedly emotional music ever created in any idiom or genre in music history. And it's all written down. A group of musicians can pick up the score and begin playing it, and all of that emotion will just spring up spontaneously. It'll come to life again one hundred years after it was written.

I was probably eight or nine when I encountered Leonard Bernstein. My parents had a record of him conducting Beethoven's *Eroica* Symphony and then giving a lecture about it with musical illustrations. Shortly after listening to that, I got the score and started studying it. *The Infinite Variety of Music* contains the text of that talk as well as other music-appreciation lectures. Bernstein was hugely important to me in terms of helping me to find a vocabulary to express what I felt about music. But at that point, I thought I was going to be some kind of towering musical-genius conductor and composer myself. I wasn't thinking about writing about music at all.

For twenty years, I've had the paperback of Wallace Stevens poems sitting on my desk. It is a totemic book for me, my first real exposure to Stevens's poetry. It's always been a habit of mine, when I feel stuck in my writing, to flip through the Stevens and reread a favorite poem. It's something to aspire to, so distant that I can never have any hope of reaching it, but when I turn back to my own writing, I find myself refreshed.

A lot of people wouldn't pick *Mythologies* as Yeats's best writing. But for me, there is something particularly magical about Yeats's prose and its rhythm. When hidden rhythms are incorporated into sentences, they can give the writing an enormous lift.

All criticism is in danger right now. So many book critics and movie critics and pop critics have lost their jobs, not just classical critics. Whether in the future there will be any magazines or newspapers with critics on staff is an open question. But as long as writers remain true to their passions and identify a language that's faithful to those passions, they will find an audience for their writing.

Stefan Sagmeister

✺— *graphic designer + typographer* —✺

These books tell a rather skimpy story: here's a guy interested in art, photography, and popular fiction. And happiness. I think the only thing that ties them all together is me.

Adolf Wölfli was a Swiss outsider artist who lived most of his life in a mental institution, working on a twenty-five-thousand-page auto-biographical epic story. His work has this incredible attention to detail; every page is filled with a kind of typographic sophistication that I find fascinating. And I have always loved Sol LeWitt's redefinition of the art-ist's role to include the program of designing a plan and having that plan executed by other people—with the end result's still being considered an original. It's amazing to think that he did his best work just before his death. As for Hiroshi Sugimoto, I'm enthralled by his ability to create true beauty by mixing formal excellence and craft with an original idea.

I grew up in a small town in the Austrian Alps. I started to write for a minor magazine called *Alphorn* when

> *I knew what I wanted: to design for the music industry and to stay small.*

I was fifteen and quickly discovered that I loved doing layout more than writing. I came to New York when I was eighteen and immediately knew that I wanted to live here. I studied at the Pratt Institute; in 1993, I launched my own design firm. I knew what I wanted: to design for the music industry and to stay small.

As a designer, I often use a process described by the Maltese philosopher Edward de Bono. He suggests starting to think about an idea for a particular project by taking a random object as a point of departure. So, let's say I have to design a pen. Instead of looking at other pens, and think-ing about how pens are used and who my target audience is, and so on and so forth, I'll consider, say—I'm in a hotel room right now—*bedspreads.*

Okay, so, hotel bedspreads are sticky, they probably have a lot of bacteria all over them—would it be possible to design a thermosensitive pen that changed colors? That could actually be nice: I'm envisioning an all-black pen that would turn yellow upon contact with the user's hand or fingers. That's what I like about de Bono's method. It forces my brain to start at a new and different point each time. It prevents me from falling into a familiar groove that I've formed before.

George Saunders

⟶ *writer* ⟶

My first job was as a geophysicist. It seemed like an active, engaged profession. I'd get to travel all over the world. The oil boom in the eighties meant that even someone with really poor grades could get a decent job overseas. Of course, in the back of my mind, I thought about writing. But I saw this Asia job as a good way to acquire some experience.

I was based in Sumatra. At night, most of the other guys would drink, and I'd occasionally join them, but more often I'd just go back to my room and write. I didn't tell anyone I was doing it. I used this really old-school typewriter, and I would just crank these things out and hide them. Mostly stories about, you know, a young American in a foreign country, stoically committing excesses, then thinking about them stoically while standing by a river or something.

But I hadn't read much of anything. I'd never read anybody except Ernest Hemingway and W. Somerset Maugham—no Hunter S. Thompson, no Jack Kerouac, no Isaac Babel. And when you don't have a resource of language to draw on, your experiences tend to get flattened out. So in real life I'd be at some crazy, brawling oil bar with all these guys like me, people from Oklahoma,

plus scuba divers from Australia, transvestites, prostitutes, drug dealers—it was like a foreign version of the bar scene in *Star Wars*. But the only thing I could write was these really terse descriptions from the point of view of some boring guy who was usually named Nick.

We would work in this camp in the jungle for four-week hitches. The camp was a forty-minute helicopter ride from the nearest city. We'd work all day and then drink all night—or, in my case, read. It was an ideal time to build a library. It was a life-or-death thing, because there was a weight limit on the helicopter for our gear, and whatever books I brought with me had to last me four weeks.

Putting together my "ideal bookshelf" was a lot like having to make those reading lists back in Sumatra. Forget any pedantic bullshit, forget trying to make my list look smarter than everybody else's—what books would I actually get off on? What would get me through those nights on the crew? I was choosing blind. *Doctor Zhivago,* John Steinbeck, *On the Road,* Aton Chekhov. Some selections would be completely ridiculous—there'd be the *Odyssey* alongside a potboiler. I had no way of distinguishing except to take them all, read them, and see what happened.

Ben Schott

—•• *writer + designer + photographer* ••—

I selected books that were either old friends or curiosities. One volume that personifies both of these traits is the gloriously misnamed compact edition of the *Oxford English Dictionary*. Each page reproduces nine pages from the non-compact version, in type so small that the book comes with its own magnifying glass with a flashlight built in. Since the *OED* is perhaps the finest reference book ever compiled, I have a slew of editions of it, including the twenty-volume monster that commandeers three and a half feet of shelving. The compact edition essentially duplicates this, but how could anyone resist a book that comes with its own bespoke magnification?

At the other end of the spectrum is this unusual copy of *Othello*. Have you ever experienced that sensation when, while ascending a flight of stairs, you clunk your foot down on a nonexistent step? Well, as I eased this volume from the shelf of a secondhand bookshop on Charing Cross Road, I sprang backward because, though it looks like a weighty tome, it's actually as light as air, being an (I presume condensed) edition in Braille. Bizarrely, there is no Braille stamping on the spine, which makes me wonder how the blind are meant to identify it.

Many of my favorite books are of this type, in some way challenging the idea of what a book can be. Which is why I have also included this volume of Dr. Shinobu Ishihara's thirty-eight plates that test for color blindness.

There is a general belief that reference books should be neutral and impersonal. But they're not. Indeed, to my mind, the best reference books are those that revel in the partial, the selective, and the personal. This is why I adore *The London Encyclopedia,* a dictionary of the city of my birth so idiosyncratic and yet so instructive that one reviewer called for it to be placed in the back of every London taxi.

Another highly personal book is *The Life of Samuel Johnson,* by James Boswell, which is almost as revealing of its author as of its subject. Nowadays more people "know" Johnson via Boswell than know the "Great Cham" through his own writings.

I'm a firm believer in thinking inside the box. The first thing I do when approaching a new project is to give myself rigid guidelines and precise limits. That's how I begin to think. If I were told that I could create anything in any medium, using any amount of space and any amount of time, I'd stand in a field and scream. Tennis needs rules, a baseline, and a net. If you could hit the ball anywhere, it would be called golf. So it goes with creativity.

The Doubtful Guest — Edward Gorey

Alexander Solzhenitsyn The Gulag Archipelago

FORTY YEARS ON AND OTHER PLAYS BY ALAN BENNETT — ff

GRAHAM GREENE * THE HUMAN FACTOR — BODLEY HEAD

ABRAM GAMES — GRAPHIC DESIGNER — Naomi Games — Catherine Moriarty — June Rose — LH

S. ISHIHARA — TESTS FOR COLOUR-BLINDNESS — 38 Plates

DYLAN THOMAS — Under Milk Wood — Dent

John Heartfield — ABRAMS

EVELYN WAUGH — Decline and Fall — Penguin

The LONDON Encyclopaedia — Edited by Ben Weinreb & Christopher Hibbert — MACMILLAN

The Compact Oxford English Dictionary — NEW EDITION — OXFORD

PG WODEHOUSE — Very Good, Jeeves

THE WIND-UP BIRD CHRONICLE — MURAKAMI — Vintage

OTHELLO

Michel Foucault — Discipline and Punish — Penguin

ff — TOM STOPPARD — Arcadia

ff — THE INTELLECTUALS AND THE MASSES — John Carey

THE LIFE OF SAMUEL JOHNSON — BOSWELL — MODERN LIBRARY

David Sedaris
⟶ *writer* ⟶

I was not a big reader in school. It wasn't until I'd dropped out of my second college and was living by myself in a trailer in a very small town in Oregon—I had a lot of time on my hands and nobody to talk to—that I got a library card and started reading. I remember reading *Babbitt,* because it had been on a list in high school. And I realized that if I didn't have to write a paper, reading was pretty fantastic. I really think you can't progress as a writer unless you read, and the ideal time to read is when you can read generously. It didn't even occur to me that I could have a book of my own in the library someday. That's how you should read.

Tobias Wolff is America's greatest living short-story writer. Sometimes I meet ministers, and I always say to them, "If I had a church, I'd read a Tobias Wolff story every week, and then I'd say to people, 'Go home.'" There's nothing else you would need to say. Every story is a manual on how to be a good person, but without ever being preachy. They're deeply moral stories; the best of them read like parables.

Raymond Carver makes writing look so easy. Every sentence has seventeen syllables and starts with the word *He*. How hard could that be? And then you realize it's pretty hard. But when I try to read a Raymond Carver story out loud, good luck. The prose is so tone-deaf. It needs more rhythm. So for me as a grownup, there's not a lot of Carver that appeals to me anymore. When I was much younger, he made writing seem so possible to me. Flannery O'Connor didn't. It does not look easy, what she comes up with. It does not look like anything that someone could sit down and come up with in an afternoon. It's always something to aspire to. If I can ever write anything as decent as one of her stories, I'll let you know. But Raymond Carver, I think he inspired a whole lot of people for that exact reason.

Dorothy Parker is someone who I'd been led to believe was funny. But I find her really sad; her stories are just really sad. "Big Blonde" is heartbreaking. And I think people find her funny because humor needs to cling to something. I used to go to these shows at Second City, and I would laugh and laugh and laugh, but then afterward I could never remember a single thing I had laughed about. I felt as if I'd had a really nice time, but I think humor needs some aspect of tragedy in order to be memorable. The funny things I remember all have a twinge of sorrow to them.

Leanne Shapton

➤➤ writer + illustrator ➤➤

These are spines that I've memorized, such as the ones on the Thomas Struth and the David Hockney, because I go back and look at those books so often. I think of books by their colors, so for me, making this bookshelf was as much an exercise in visual memory as it was a challenge to remember the contents inside.

When I was little, my mother would give me one M&M for every book I read. I'd have to read ten books just to get a decent mouthful of chocolate. So I'd go to the library and check out this huge pile of books. I'd stack them up on my left, go through them one by one, and then restack them on my right. Then I'd bring my mother the pile of books to tally, demanding my chocolate.

My mother would give me one M&M for every book I read. I'd have to read ten books for a decent mouthful of chocolate.

My father gave me the Jim McMullan book when I was fourteen. He used to go to government surplus auctions, where he'd buy things like coffee tables and Dodge vans, and one day he found this book at an auction and brought it home. I remember going through it and copying the watercolors. That book was my introduction to artistic practice; after that, I began to think about illustration more seriously. Eventually I went on to assist Jim in New York, so that's probably the oldest book on this shelf.

All the Clothes of a Woman is by Hans-Peter Feldmann. The entire book consists of these grainy black and white photographs of a woman's wardrobe: a lonely pair of tights, some ski boots, a pair of jeans, a bra, a turtleneck. Feldmann saw beauty in these very normal, lumpy, faded clothes. I find it so honest and romantic. I think that's how we want to be loved as women.

I really like Jo Ann Beard's tiny, tiny moments. There's an ending in one of her essays where she looks down and notices that her shorts are bagging out. And it's such a minuscule observation, but that really is how and what we see during profound or important moments in our lives. Her writing changed the way I thought about nonfiction.

Sally Singer

—➤ editor ➤—

There was a way in which Grace Paley described young womanhood in New York and in a Jewish family that really connected with me when I was quite young. I think I saw myself as a Grace Paley character. If you were to ask me why, though, I wouldn't have an answer. I also loved the idea of spending a season in London. I don't come from the sort of family whose members spend a season in London—I grew up in California—but for some reason, I always felt like I should be a Mitford sister.

I'm not a writer, I'm an editor. I have always been an editor. I love pushing it just enough to take readers some-place they didn't know they were going to go. And I see patterns—in pictures, in text, in fashion, in everything. I see narratives everywhere.

There's a way in which these books—if you read fiction critically and emotionally and consistently your whole life—allow you access to visions of yourself. They give you all the themes you want to play out. They give you a glimpse of other lives. There are certain writers on this shelf who talk about uncomfortable times, who use language with a lot of control to describe upsetting situations. I love Flannery O'Connor and Leonard Michaels for that reason. I remember when I first discovered Tom Robbins

and the kind of goofy playfulness in his work. His books aren't great literature, if you ask me, but they have a kind of vibrancy and brashness that I found liberating.

Everyone has his or her taste. I think some people have an eye—whether for design, for art, or for narrative—that is more refined than others' eyes just because of what they've read and looked at and how they've trained themselves to see things. Then there are people who are more intuitive: they just *know*. They may not know why it matters, but they can see something in the proportions or the shape of a narrative, of a dress, of a chair. They can see the shift, where culture moves.

And I think it comes from feeling intensely awkward in the world. From feeling at right angles to what is considered articulate, popular, and beautiful—whatever is valued in the dominant culture. It might all just be in your own head—it probably is—but your own head is a vast region. And you try to find ways of presenting yourself in order to make the business of getting up, going out, and being part of things easier.

> *I see patterns—in pictures, in text, in fashion, in everything. I see narratives everywhere.*

Nadia Sirota

— violist —

There's something about the voice of the viola that's very attractive to me. On a violin, the ratio of string length to body is pretty much perfect. But the viola is so out of proportion. It should be the size of a small cello. You really have to work to get the sound of the string going. It sounds like a man singing very high or a woman singing very low. It's not really comfortable in its own body.

When I was first asked to do this, I thought I should pick fourteen copies of *Colors Insulting to Nature*. That is a book you can read alone on the train and pee yourself laughing at. It's about America's obsession with fame. The protagonist is this completely talentless girl whose mother is trying to push her into a career of wealth and celebrity. My friend Nico Muhly gave it to me. He bought seven copies on Amazon and started handing them out as party favors. I've never wanted a book to be a movie as badly as I do this one, not because I think it'd translate very well, but because I want more than anything to experience it at the *same time* as other people. The only extremely frustrating thing about *Colors Insulting to Nature* is that you're at it alone. But that's fine. It's still great.

I went through a period where I read jockishly, if that makes sense. I read a ton of Pynchon. I'm not sure I enjoyed any of it. It was intellectual sports, the equivalent of boasting, "Check out what I can bench-press!" I was interested in coming across as impenetrable. I was forever smoking cigarettes on the steps of my school with a scowl on my face. But that was the reason I completely lost my mind when I read *Infinite Jest*. Here was a dense, grown-up contemporary novel in which every single moment is absolutely enjoyable. The older I get, the more I think my taste has shifted. Now I read for fun.

Our Band Could Be Your Life is about the DIY aspect of the postpunk indie music scene in the eighties, which I think has so many parallels to the new classical scene right now. We're thriving in the eyes of the press, which is really unbelievable, considering that we're making music on such a small scale and without any infrastructure. So I find that book encouraging, because it's about a bunch of people who successfully created a movement out of nothing. Classical music is in a weird place at the moment. So much of it is completely crumbling in the most gigantic way. Even if you're doing the most saleable thing, like the Tchaikovsky Violin Concerto with the New York Philharmonic, there's no guarantee it'll do well. There is room to do things differently.

Aria Beth Sloss

writer

What interested me about this exercise was that I had to have an organizing principle to limit my selection, because there are too many books that I love. Too many books full of powerful, elegant sentences. Every one of these writers—from Andrew Sean Greer to Nabokov to Virginia Woolf—writes sentences that could fell you. That's what I've always focused on when I'm reading, the sentences.

Every one of these writers—from Andrew Sean Greer to Nabokov to Virginia Woolf—writes sentences that could fell you.

But I had to really ask myself, Which books have changed my perception of what a book can be? Maybe that's more a fiction writer's question, the question of what a book *is*. I felt pretentious putting *Ulysses* on my shelf, but I had to do it. I still remember the experience of reading it: I was in this state of complete wonder. I couldn't believe it was a novel. I had an idea in my head of what a novel was, and that book cracked my idea wide open. So this shelf is an extension of that moment, that kind of violent revelation. Every book on it reminds me that writing is an act of invention.

Patti Smith

musician + poet + artist

As a child, I would sit at my mother's feet and watch her drink coffee and smoke cigarettes with a book on her lap. Her absorption intrigued me. Although not yet in nursery school, I liked to look at her books, feel their paper, and lift the tissues from their frontispieces. I wanted to know what was in them, what captured her attention so deeply.

I longed to read everything I possibly could, and the things I read in turn produced new yearnings.

When my mother discovered that I had hidden her crimson copy of Foxe's *Book of Martyrs* beneath my pillow, in hopes of absorbing its meaning, she sat me down and began the laborious process of teaching me to read. With great effort, we moved through Mother Goose and on to Dr. Seuss. When I advanced past the need for instruction, I was permitted to join her on our overstuffed sofa, she reading *The Shoes of the Fisherman* and I *The Red Shoes*. . . . I was completely smitten by that book. I longed to read everything I possibly could, and the things I read in turn produced new yearnings.

Alec Soth

— *photographer* —

I live in Minnesota, and while it's not exactly life on the tundra here, there isn't a gallery on every corner, either. So as a youngster, I got my visual culture through books and magazines. Books especially were the primary medium by which to access photography. I still cherish my copy of *Summer Nights* by Robert Adams, even though it has this incredibly cheesy cover. I still remember when I first found it, and I credit it as one of the great discoveries that made me want to be a photographer.

You have to imagine the great journey you're on in order to make your own bookshelf.

The colored books are Paul Graham's multi-volume work *A Shimmer of Possibility*. I put them on my shelf for two reasons. First, I thought they'd be fun to paint. Second, and more important, taken together, they comprise the best photography book published in the last ten years. As a collection, it makes me jealous; it's the book I have to contend with as a photographer. For me, to include it here was to say, "Okay, you won. You produced the best book. It's better than I'll ever do." Paul Graham has taken classic street photography and given it a certain cinematic quality. Each volume is almost like a separate short story, presenting a sequence of actions—for example, one shows a man smoking a cigarette while someone walks by on the street. The series deals with time in a way that's totally different from what we're used to seeing. And it achieves something in books that couldn't be achieved in any other medium. That's very important to me as a photographer: I want to make great books. I want to have great shows, too, but in many ways, a show is secondary to a great book.

The Alice Neel and Lucien Freud books represent a moment in my life when I wanted to be a painter. I felt a lot of grief when I gave up my painting aspirations. It took a while. But it was a key part of that path for me. The thing is, it's not like there's some set way of becoming who you are. You don't have to do the BFA, the semester in Paris, the MFA, the teaching job. These books on my shelf are linked to different moments of my life. You have to imagine the great journey you're on in order to make your own bookshelf. Start with what your mom used to read you, the book you used to chew on as a toddler, and just keep building from there.

Scott Spencer
writer

All writers say this: I was an avid and enthusiastic reader, and there was a world out there that was better than the world I lived in, and I thought I could one day be a part of that. Which is why I chose that old *Evergreen Review*. The place where I was raised was just a little postwar development in the far South Side of Chicago; my father worked in steel mills, and the people who lived around us were bus drivers and cops and manual laborers. The *Evergreen Review* gave me the idea of some dazzling bohemia that I would one day be a part of.

In high school, the form of my rebellion was political. I was involved in the Student Peace Union; I was a member of CORE, fighting the police, fighting the state. I'm happy about that and proud of that, but it wasn't really nourishing to writing. In politics, you're either for or against something; in writing, you're much more involved in nuance. Reading *Letting Go* slowed me down; it showed me the richness of exploring internal life, of moral ambiguity.

I picked up *Revolutionary Road* because I thought it was about the Marxist revolution. As in Hemingway, there is a clarity of the sentence in Yates's book; there is no shine, no dazzle. He also writes about what was my own greatest fear as a young person, that none of my dreams would come true. I didn't want to end up working in an office, being one of those people with a manuscript stashed away in their bottom drawer. I didn't want to tell people I was writing a novel, and have them keep asking me about it, and be cast into a barren silence. I was writing my first book as if it were possibly against the law.

The Cheever was given to me by the mother of a girl I went out with in high school. I was filled with scorn for it. All I knew about John Cheever was that he lived in Westchester and wrote about the suburbs—why would I ever, ever, ever want to read about something like that? And then to discover how wrong I'd been, to realize just how mystical that writer was and how magical and otherworldly his vision of life was, it was such a strong corrective to my youthful knee-jerk dismissal. It opened me up to the poetry of everyday life.

A book is a relationship between a writer and a reader. The meaning changes from reader to reader. Somebody who used my shelf as a reading list to find out what fiction can do would be in pretty good shape.

Lorin Stein

—•→ *editor* ←•—

I became an English major because I took a seminar with John Hollander. One day, after the seminar was over, I bumped into him on the street. We were making chitchat, and finally he said, "Come to my office tomorrow, and I'll try to keep you from wasting the rest of your time in college."

The reading list he gave me was that two-volume *Oxford Anthology.* He was one of the editors. He told me to read it over my summer break. It happened to be the same anthology that we'd been assigned in my high school. So I went back and this time I actually read it—and discovered that Nicky Kaill, who sat next to me in tenth-grade English class, had written I AM SUPERIOR in magic marker across the first seventy-five pages of volume I.

I wanted to be a writer, but I wasn't any good at it. I read *Infinite Jest* and gave up. So I thought I would try to make a living as a book critic. That was my plan after college. I remember calling up the *Washington Post* book reviewer, whom I didn't know, and asking him how I might go about doing that. He told me it was a dumb idea. I tried to get a job at a magazine where a cousin of mine worked, and he said there was no way he would hire me. But he also advised me that I could sit and read as many books or magazines as I wanted for free at Barnes & Noble. This was pretty new information at the time. *Granta* had just come out with its first list of the best young American writers; I worked my way through that. I tried to read two or three books a week. Eventually I got a secretarial job at *Publishers Weekly.* That was where I started editing professionally.

Is there an important job to be done at the *Paris Review*? I think so. There's a certain kind of story or poem or essay that keeps making its way into my head. Put it this way: when Walter Benjamin was young, he tried to translate a few short poems by Baudelaire. The result was *The Arcades Project,* which was already a thousand pages long when Benjamin died. Those were just his translator's notes. The reason it took Benjamin so long to start dealing with Baudelaire's little poems was that Baudelaire had been there, paying attention, at the birth of mass society. Because of that, Benjamin said, Baudelaire understood the world we live in, whereas the rest of us don't. We have to read his poems to get it. I want to find new writing that provides that same feeling, that registers the changes we've all lived through, that we're living through, or that we've just inherited.

John Jeremiah Sullivan
writer

I'm thinking of things that could actually sustain me over time. That's what comes to mind when I hear the phrase "ideal bookshelf." I'm imagining that the end of the world has happened, and I'm living on a small boat in the Pacific with only my family and the few people I was able to chopper out of various locations, and this is the crude plank shelf by the hammock in which I will probably die—no doubt mere days before my shipmates wash up on a radiation-free island where they can restart society. So I want to have deep books, life books, nothing that anyone could ever tire of.

Strangely, I don't want the Bible. The King James English is magnificent, but the stories, I don't know: I've never really felt they were as great as everybody says, except where they're really disturbing and scarring, and I think the future can do without them. I want Guy Davenport's *7 Greeks,* mainly for the Heraclitus and the Sappho. That can be the new Bible on the island.

I want Edith Wharton's *Old New York,* just to have a couple of examples of dense aesthetic perfection. That's one reading experience of which I remember coming to the end and thinking, I wouldn't have changed a comma of that. It is just so fully realized.

The Life of Samuel Johnson is a whole world unto itself. (The collected works of Shakespeare are, too, but there wouldn't be room for them.) Boswell is endless. It reads differently every time. Johnson said it himself: "When a man is tired of London, he is tired of life." You could say the exact same thing about that book: if you ever got sick of James Boswell, then you'd know you were probably really depressed. He's both gossipy and great. He's noticing and recording everything Johnson does. He has the courage to recognize his place in the project, to be a professional sycophant. He isn't pretending to be anything else. And as a result, we have Johnson.

There should also be something really funny on my boat shelf, for those inevitable despair sessions. *Henry IV,* parts one and two, mainly for Falstaff. I'd want a good children's story, to keep the young people literate: *The Swiss Family Robinson,* in the old nineteenth-century translation. And a blank book, a journal—a big fat one for writing in, to record reactions to the books and favorite quotations. And births and deaths out on the boat.

Of course, when I start thinking about all I'm leaving out, I get a drowning feeling, but I believe this would be a decent shelf from which to regrow civilization.

Christina Tosi

—• *baker + cookbook author* •—

I have a really big sweet tooth. My grandmothers baked, my mother baked, and I followed suit. I love eating sweets as much as I love the nurturing aspect of baking for someone else. But I didn't think of doing it for a living at first. I was very good at math, and someone told me I should be an engineer. So I went through my first year of college studying to become an electrical engineer.

Craig Claiborne's *New York Times Cookbook* and *The Joy of Cooking* were the two cookbooks from my mom's kitchen that I took with me when I left for college. My mom is a funny baker. She is a professional woman who worked eighty hours a week, but she also grew up as one of five kids in a family from rural Ohio. She's of that down-home mentality where you cook, you bake, every day for every occasion, even just a weekday dinner.

A lot of what I do at Momofuku Milk Bar is drawn from the baking I did at home with my practical, don't-take-yourself-so-seriously mom. The stock in the kitchen is what you'd find in almost anyone's pantry: cornflakes, bananas, pretzels, mini chocolate chips, yellow cake mix. At Milk Bar, we don't actually make cakes out of yellow cake mix, but we'll use it in recipes for frosting or ice cream because its flavor is so significant in people's

closely held memories of food. Of course, we inevitably go through a series of complicated steps to make something that is seemingly simple—we make caramelized cornflakes, for example, with butter, salt, sugar, cornflakes, and milk powder. Homing in on those familiar, sentimental flavors and presenting them to people in a way that's clever or thoughtful but still "getable" is the real art form at our restaurant.

That's what makes a truly good dessert on any level, if you ask me—even at a four-star dining establishment. It should remind you of something you know. We always have massive jugs of Ovaltine on hand because when you taste something that's been flavored with chocolate and malt, you remember it, it takes you back, it's familiar. If you're a small business owner in New York City, the only way you're going to survive is by being as handy and resourceful as possible. That's why I have *The Complete Do-It-Yourself Manual* on my shelf. We forget about the simpler ways to get things done, from roasting a chicken to fixing a bike chain. Figuring out how to make stuff work taps into the creative part of my head the same way baking does. For me, it's not just about turning out a fantastic layer cake. It's about being creative in everything I do.

Wells Tower

—➤ *writer* ➤—

Each one of these books is here to remind me that a different kind of work is possible in fiction. I read Charles Portis in order to remember that a flat, curt sentence can be absolutely hilarious. Yasunari Kawabata offers a reminder not to live in fear of beauty. Kawabata's beauty is never a sentimental gesture, it's always compositional, but it's so far outside my own psychology that it's great for me to dip into it from time to time. *Mrs. Bridge* is a caution to keep chapters short. There's a way in which Evan S. Connell gets to a deep and upsetting place with very tidy and measured brushstrokes. It's a comfort to know that a writer can achieve that without ever appearing to strive for it.

When I was first starting out, I thought it must be possible to take apart a Richard Yates short story almost mathematically: *If you have two paragraphs of expository information about the characters, and the characters are in this kind of relationship, and if you expose them to an incident of this approximate shape, then that's a successful story.* It was a disastrous thing to try to replicate—you can't crack someone else's formula—but I keep Yates's stories around because I admire their architectural rigor.

I have a weird relationship with *The Four Quartets.* After graduate school, I moved up to my grandparents'

summer house in Maine. I thought I'd get a lot of writing done there, but I couldn't handle the solitude. There was something about the land, too, that inspired in me a weird obsession with the third quartet, entitled "The Dry Salvages," which is about time and the sea and the rocky New England landscape. I think by some point I had memorized all four of the quartets, which is just an embarrassingly pretentious amount of poetry to have committed to memory. But the rote task of memorizing had a calming effect on me.

I tend to cite Barry Hannah's instructions for writing a short story: "Get in and get out." Facile, maybe, but it's a good plan to keep in mind when you're stuck: cut your way to an exit. Probably the most useful writing advice of all comes from "Politics in the English Language," in which George Orwell talks about the need always to make sure that the language is in direct service to an idea or an image, and never to let the words get away from you. That's why Orwell is on this shelf. Of course, Barry Hannah is a countermanding voice because language is forever getting away from him. There's some pleasure in that, too.

Gina Trapani
app developer

When my mother was a kid, she discovered that my grandmother was illiterate. My mom would ask my grandmother to check her homework, and my grandmother would always say it looked great, even when there were obvious mistakes in it. So my mom became suspicious. It affected her so profoundly that she later became a reading teacher. And she instilled in me, at a very young age, the notion that literacy meant independence. I have no doubt that that's why I turned into such a bookworm.

I picked up *Clan of the Cave Bear* when I was seven. I had made this decision in my early childhood that I would read every single book in existence. That way, I would know everything, I thought. It was my personal Mount Everest. And though that book was wildly age-inappropriate for me—it has scenes of rape, sex, and violence—I ate it up. So I decided to be bold and write a book report on it for school. My teacher wrote across the top, "Counts for two book reports." My classmates were so envious.

I romanticized the idea that anything bound in a book had to be true knowledge. And there came a point when I discovered that wasn't true. It was a really horrifying revelation, but also a relief. There were so many books; I knew it'd be impossible for me to read them all.

Getting Things Done was one of the seeds that started Lifehacker. It's a personal productivity book. David Allen was targeting corporate executives, but in 2004, his ideas struck a chord with the programmer-coder community. Allen talks about this methodology—and engineers *love* methodology—of setting up buckets so that information will flow logically from one to the next. Software started popping up that would help you implement the GTD protocols (we called the book *GTD* for short). After that, this idea for life hacks began to float around the Web. And we launched lifehacker.com in 2005.

Night by Eli Wiesel is here because of my father. One day, when I was a junior in college, he went to work, came home, and died of a heart attack. I was barely functional after that. My grades took a dive. And I chose to take a class on the literature of the Holocaust. We read *Night,* which is about a teenage son and his father at a concentration camp, and it laid me bare. Reading that book was my grieving process for my father. It was a semester-long funeral, for sure. I don't look back at that time with either fondness or nostalgia, but it's important to know that there are books that can guide you through a series of emotions that you don't want to feel on your own.

Jakob Trollbäck

— ◆ designer ◆ —

I grew up in Sweden. I worked as a waiter next door to a record store, and then I was offered a job there, and I became interested in music. I began to DJ, and through being a DJ, I got involved with a gallery. We did Saturday parties at the gallery, and I put together the mailers and fliers and stuff like that. We rented a movie theater and started a club where we mounted art shows. We had movie screenings and the best parties.

> *I think that ultimately, evolution is about transformation, and creativity is a necessary force for evolution.*

Around that time I also got a computer and was doing more design work, and I thought, Well, maybe I should be a graphic designer. The idea came as something of a surprise. But I think these different connections explain why I like the Swiss graphic designer Josef Müller Brockman. He's famous for his posters, most of which were commissioned for music concerts. He's Swiss and strict with his designs, but there is still so much motion in his work: you can see an internal dialogue going on in there about static and kinetic energy. He always creates a snapshot of something with a lot of movement in it.

These books are about transformation. I think that ultimately, evolution is about transformation, and creativity is a necessary force for evolution. It's how we figure out how to do things differently. Gerhard Richter is a fantastic example of this, which is why he's on this shelf. He's always saying things like, "I don't know what the big fuss is about, I just take a photograph that I like, project it onto a canvas, and paint it." But something happens in that transformation: it makes you question what you've seen. It changes your perspective. It can be as small a shift as looking at Richter's work and mistaking a painting for a photograph. I think that's what we're also trying to do in both our commercial and our noncommercial projects: find transformative moments.

Robert Verdi

I grew up an average-to-poor kid in Maplewood, New Jersey. My parents are Portuguese immigrants; I'm a first-generation American. There were kids in my high school who would get a Mercedes or a Porsche for their birthday. And I had to save up from mowing lawns to buy a $700 1978 orange Rabbit. At sixteen, I started working at Bloomingdale's. When I got my first commission check, for $1,110, I went and bought an Armani cardigan.

Armani was just hitting the United States then, and the label was all the buzz: Armani, Armani, Armani. The next day, I put on my new cardigan and went in to work early, purposely creating my own "lady's mile" so that I could prance around the mall. And people responded to me differently, because suddenly I looked like a whole other person. I wasn't really any different, but my affectation had changed because of this sweater. And I realized at that moment that I could manipulate people with fashion; I could play the rich kid even though I wasn't that at all. Fashion is a way to inform others about who you are, or who you want to be, without even opening your mouth.

Fashion is a way to inform others about who you are, or who you want to be, without even opening your mouth.

For me, a book is something I can touch. An image on the computer screen doesn't exist, really; it's just a bunch of pixels. Sure, I can come back to it, but I think most often we forget about the stuff that we bookmark online. A book is tangible evidence of a life. And I love what books add to a physical environment: they give a room depth and texture, as well as good karma, I think. Books seep into the atmosphere of a room.

Vendela Vida
writer

I like to keep these books near me. I don't open them that often—I can't say I frequently turn to a line in the *Inferno,* for example. But I like to have the physical objects near me as reassurance, as a reminder that they exist, that I live in a world where they were created. They're like lifelong friends to me; I need to know they're there, even if I don't check in with them on a regular basis.

Out of all of these books, I've probably reread *Disgrace* the most times. In my opinion, it's the perfect novel. It works on so many levels—personal, sexual, political— and of course, it's masterfully written. The first line of it is fantastic: "For a man of his age, fifty-two, divorced, he has, to his mind, figured out the problem of sex rather well." Of course, the second time you read the book, you read it with the knowledge that he hasn't figured out the problem of sex at all—and that line becomes tragic and funny at the same time.

I think Mary McCarthy and Joan Didion are immediately appealing when you're starting out as a writer. There's also something about each of their styles of writing that makes it look deceptively simple to emulate. Their books are ethereal and specific at the same time, which is a really interesting combination, and one that's very difficult to achieve. Both women's writing possesses this amazing gritty grace, no matter what they're writing about, and I turned to their books countless times when I was in my early twenties and living in New York. I moved so often in those early years and lent those books out to so many people (who never gave them back) that I've had to buy the paperbacks ten times over.

I read the *Inferno* when I was living in Italy. I remember the ending so well: Dante and Virgil come up through the bottom of the Earth, through hell, and emerge "to see once more the stars." I thought that was such an interesting view of the world—that you could go so deep into it that you would have to come out a different way. In my twenties, I tried to write a novel loosely inspired by the *Inferno.* The working title was *To See Once More the Stars.*

Why do I write? In some ways, for the same reasons that I read: to know I'm not alone. But that's not the full explanation. Books have had more influence on me than anything else in my life, and I turn to them for everything: escape, humor, philosophy, story, and craft. I write because I can't not write. Literature holds so much power over me, it has whispered in my ear so often, that I have to respond.

Ayelet Waldman
➤ *writer* ➤

I remember the first Jane Austen book I read. It was *Pride and Prejudice,* and I must have been in seventh or eighth grade. I was going through a Gothic and Regency Romance phase, which drove my feminist mother crazy. I would go to the library and check out one Barbara Cartland bodice ripper after another. A savvy librarian took pity on my long-suffering mother and slipped me a copy of *Pride and Prejudice*. The cover looked exactly the same as those on the books I was used to reading, except that the heroine was perhaps a bit flatter-chested. With the first page, I was hooked, and I immediately read everything else by Jane Austen as well. *Persuasion* immediately became, and remains, my favorite.

What Dave Eggers accomplishes in *What Is the What* is truly astonishing: he inhabits a character who could not be more different from him, and does it with absolute authenticity. To read this novel is to take a master class in character. Dave's book stands as my inspiration for how far a gifted writer can go.

I became a writer because I failed at being a stay-at-home mother. After my eldest child was born, I went back to work as a public defender almost at once. My husband stayed home with the baby. They were together all day,

a team of two, having so much fun. He would take her for walks, to story time at the library. And there I'd be, pumping breast milk in the parking lot of the Metropolitan Detention Center on my way in to visit clients who were facing ten-year mandatory minimum sentences for minor drug crimes. I decided to quit work and join my husband and daughter in their idyllic life.

After completing less than three days of full-time baby care, however, I began to lose my mind. I knew I had to find something to do independent of being a mom. I was a huge fan of murder mysteries, and like all fans, I had read both great and terrible examples of the genre. It occurred to me that I could try to write a mystery of my own; surely it would be no worse than some of the bad ones I'd read. The Mommy Track Mysteries that I ended up writing were my MFA. They taught me not only how to write but how to be a disciplined writer who gets her work done.

I know that I'll never be as great a novelist as the artists on my fantasy bookshelf. I'll never be Edward St. Aubyn, or my husband. I'll never be Jane Austen. But I hope that I'll always continue to improve, and that each of my novels will be better than its predecessors.

Alice Waters

chef + cookbook author

Elizabeth David's was my first cookbook. I went to France when I was in college, for a semester abroad, and I returned a complete Francophile. It was an awakening for me: I felt as if I had never really eaten before that trip. And upon my return, someone told me to read Elizabeth David. I fell in love with the way she thought about food, the way she tasted food, the way she wrote about food. I cooked everything in that book. Her writing eventually led me to Richard Olney, and later to Diana Kennedy and Edna Lewis. I think all of their ideas played a part in making me want to create a place like Chez Panisse, and they still influence my restaurant today.

I encountered Niloufer Ichaporia King and William Rubel later, but their books are dear to me for very similar reasons. It's all about the hearth, about the fire. And, of course, the wine—you can't forget the wine, which is why Kermit Lynch's books are on my shelf, too. He is someone who thinks very much about the soil, about *terroir,* about letting the irregularities of the wine stand for what they are, letting that be part of the experience. And I think that's something we aspire to at Chez Panisse as well: we try never to mask ingredients or change them into something they're not.

I once cooked for M. F. K. Fisher, on her seventieth birthday. Her writing is so imaginative; I've often tried to cook a meal just from the way she wrote about it. And I think that says something, too, about what I hope to do: it's about getting at the essence of something.

I've always thought of food as an aesthetic experience, and of a meal as a chance to meditate on what's on the plate, and how the plate is arranged, and where everything comes from. But once you begin to think like that, you begin to ask questions, and then you begin to look for answers—from the farmer, from the earth. Which of course leads into the writing of Wendell Berry and Michael Pollan, whose books are here, too. And eventually that takes you to the classroom, which is why I've included *Fast Food Nation* and Jonathan Kozol on my shelf.

Other books here are about opening the senses, whether through Maira Kalman's sense of humor or Olafur Eliasson's art. Food, I think, can do that very simply, very humbly, and without much embellishment. Because at the end of the day, it's just as David Tanis says: All we want to eat is a plate of figs. That's it: a plate of figs.

William Wegman

—•— *artist* —•—

These books correspond to my childhood. They capture how I think of myself then: walking through the woods, climbing trees, looking at leaves, and digging holes. Back in the fifties, it was a safer time—or at least people thought it was. Our mothers would let us go out, let us hitchhike, let us drive off with friends. There was so much freedom to wander. I was always in the woods, building huts and sleeping outside. I had a dog growing up, so he would come with me, too. His name was Wags; he was a mutt. He lived to be twenty, and he was a good dog. These books are nostalgic for me. That's the spell.

I remember reading the Hardy Boys books by the light of a flashlight under the covers because I wasn't allowed to stay up late. And I was really attracted to those picture encyclopedias. I'd draw from them as a kid. My parents told me that I would fall asleep every night with volumes on my chest.

My father completed only the tenth grade. His father was killed when he was young, so all of the younger brothers worked to support the older ones who went off to college. It was unfair, but that was what happened. My mother won a scholarship to Pratt, but her father wouldn't let her go, because girls from Massachusetts just didn't move to New York City. My father is in his nineties now; he lives in the house where my sister and I grew up. He's a very sweet person who, thankfully, let me do what I wanted to do. When I said I wanted to go to art school, it was fine with him.

It was my high school art teacher who told me to go. I'd taken art in the first place only because I needed an A for my college applications, and I knew I'd get one in that class. It was a close call: I didn't really think about having a career as an artist. A job doing illustrating or something, sure, why not? But fine art was not part of our vocabulary.

My father, for instance, used to make us these trophies for special occasions. They were like sculptures, and if they'd been displayed in a gallery, critics would have written about them as art. But my father would never have done that. He would never have called them art himself. I think it can be terrifying to call yourself an artist, to give yourself artistic license. But if they'd just allow themselves to surrender to it, I'm sure a lot of people would be.

George Weld

•• chef + farmer ••

Marcella Hazan's *Essentials of Classic Italian Cooking* was a cookbook I read like a novel when I first got it. I cooked out of it exclusively for two years. I wanted Marcella Hazan to adopt me. Her tone is very stern and demanding—"If you want to make gnocchi, it must be done this way," that sort of thing—and I sucked it up. I studied poetry before I became a cook, and there was something satisfying

All this time, I've been wishing I'd been born Italian and complaining about not having a culinary tradition. But as a Southerner, I have a huge tradition.

about following Marcella's directions. Every time I made food according to a recipe of hers, it turned out perfectly. It was so different from sitting in a class taught by Robert Pinsky, where we'd all go on and on about what might or might not make a poem work.

I wanted to be Italian. I tried to study Italian. My wife and I spent our honeymoon in Italy. I watched every Italian movie I could. All these superficial, dumb things. I got really into Italian poets. And then I had this moment. I was at home, looking at my mother's recipe box—she was not an inspired cook in any way—and I realized it had my great-grandmother's recipes in it, recipes she had inherited. And it was this flash of realization: All this time, I've been wishing I'd been born Italian and complaining about not having a culinary tradition. But as a Southerner, I have a huge tradition. We had a farm in Virginia when I was little, and we had a smokehouse, and I remember we could still smell that smoke in the old bones hanging from the rafters. I think I base a lot of my tradition on the idea of that smoke. So in a roundabout way, Hazan really changed how I thought about food. I began to relate to it as an expression of tradition. Everything I ever wished that Marcella Hazan could give me, I have.

Megan Whitmarsh

artist

I lived in France when I was little for a couple of years. My parents were trying to learn the language, so we all read *Tintin*. I have such incredibly vivid memories of *Tintin*—I *know* it has influenced my art and the way I think about things. I'm really detail-oriented, for example, and if you look at *Tintin,* you'll see that even a drawing of a vase is superintricate. I love Hergé's palette. I even started doing calisthenics every morning because I wanted to exercise more and had this vague memory of Tintin's touching his toes. I thought, Perfect! I will wake up and touch my toes each day!

My favorite author is Clarice Lispector. She's a writer who illuminates what I sense but don't always know how to articulate. She describes how an artist is attempting to do something and continually failing and how that's okay because art is like life, it's a process rather than an end. She once said writing was like trying to photograph perfume. You're hoping to pin something down that is mutable. I think about that when I'm making art. I have to approach it sideways; if I get too calculated, that's when I produce predictable work.

From among my peers I picked Christopher Forgues's *Powr Mastrs.* He makes comics, but they're totally art. I love the cryptic beauty of his drawings and narratives. I was introduced to Christopher's work when he sent me a fan letter for this comic I used to do called *Snow Monkeys.* For a long time I had this very provincial idea that real art had to be serious, like oil painting or something. My work at school was divided into "art" on the one hand and things I had more fun making, like comics, on the other. But in making those comics, I realized that they had a certain kind of energy that was missing in my other art. And so I began to take more risks with it. It feels more integrated now. Although I haven't made comics in years, I still love their language. It's freeing.

I want the things that I surround myself with to radiate optimism and love. It sounds cheesy, but it's true. I believe that if people can speak fearlessly from their hearts, that genuineness will radiate, and those around them will start to trust themselves and investigate their own inner workings—which is how we connect with others in a positive way. These are the books I surround myself with and feel inspired by. Maybe if others read them, they will find a similar inspiration to be optimistic and listen to their own voices. That would be a cool result.

Henry Sene Yee

book cover designer

People who work in design like to have objects around them. When I was little, my mom used to call me Monkey because I would never stop jumping around. The toy zebra was a gift; I don't have that much of a personal connection to zebras, but they're an animal ideally suited to graphic design. Before I attended the School of Visual Arts, I saw a poster on the subway promoting the school: it showed a zebra, but instead of black and white stripes, it had rainbow stripes. The tagline beneath it read: "To be good is not enough when you dream of being great." And I thought, Yeah, okay, I can get into that.

I graduated from the School of Visual Arts in the late eighties. The hottest job around in those days was working on twelve-inch album covers. But the industry was undergoing massive change, shifting from analog vinyl to digital CDs, and it changed the whole field. Now books are changing in much the same way.

I fell into books by accident. I was freelancing for Louise Fili, the art director at Pantheon, but I planned to stay there only until a record job opened up. She was interviewing some of my classmates, and I asked her what was going on. She told me she was looking for an assistant, and she knew I wasn't interested. I quickly said, "Yes, I am." It must have been my jealousy and competitive nature speaking, but I've been in books ever since. It's been about twenty years now.

I designed the covers for two of the books on here—*Middlesex* and *The Amazing Adventures of Kavalier & Clay* are my designs. Even if I'd had nothing to do with creating those covers, I would still love them for my own reasons. The books were published years ago, but people still respond to their covers, and I'm proud of them. Sometimes I will look at my old work and be embarrassed. But I know that I always did the best job given what I knew at the moment, so I can still remain proud. I think that's true for any creative process.

I don't want to overanalyze my choices for my bookshelf. I'm not trying to be someone else. My likes are different than your likes; we each just have to own that. It's like my love of dark chocolate: I can't explain it. I love good stories, wherever they may come from—books, films, conversations. These books are not here to project or display who I am or who I'm trying to be. They are just a snapshot of what I want close to me.

Jonathan Zittrain

— ⟶ *legal scholar + professor* ⟵ —

It would be an understatement to say that I was a big nerd as a teenager. In the eighties, I signed on to CompuServe as a twelve-year-old. Ran up a huge bill. And when my parents saw it, they were like, "That's it, no more . . . *whatever* that is." When I logged in to say I couldn't afford it anymore, I was instead given free time on the service for pitching in. I became an assistant "sysop," or system operator. This was during an era where sysops could actually govern their online zones by fiat. When people acted out, the sysop could delete their messages and throw them out of the forum, and they couldn't come back. And it was

> *If I'm on a desert island with a single bookshelf, the first thing I'm going to want to do after finding a can opener is (re)build an Internet.*

really interesting to try to think through how to be fair rather than despotic in that capacity. I think my interest in law stems from similar questions about how communities can fairly govern themselves.

Internetworking with TCP/IP is on this shelf because TCP/IP is a thing of beauty. There's not a Nobel Prize for its category of contribution, so the book can't win one; it's also got so many authors that the committee wouldn't know whom to invite to Sweden for the ceremony. But I have found the features and tradeoffs represented by that protocol to be a powerful metaphor for governance with maximally distributed authority. It's totally counterintuitive at first. But if I'm on a desert island with a single bookshelf, the first thing I'm going to want to do after finding a can opener is (re)build an Internet.

So much of *Catch-22* is about the casualties of bureaucracy. It's about the systems we build to govern ourselves, and how they become so manifestly absurd that we can't escape them. Of course, it's a cautionary tale as well; it's about what happens when a system, even one that has a flow to it, loses its humanity.

I guess one lesson I could draw from compiling this list is that your calling, if you've actually got one, will find you. The books on my shelf all point in a certain direction for me, even though I encountered them in very different phases of my life. And given that they have so much in common, they may also serve as a reminder not to make the ideal bookshelf your *only* bookshelf. It's important to leave enough space for other books, ones that don't always line up like iron filings. Let the shelf build itself.

Contributors and Their Books

Hugh Acheson is the chef and partner of Five & Ten, The National, Gosford Wine, and Empire State South. He is based in Athens, Georgia.

Cider Beans, Wild Greens, and Dandelion Jelly; Southern Belly; Terrines, Pâtés & Galantines; Classic French Cooking [Elisabeth Luard]; *Tender; Culinary Artistry; Larousse Gastronomique; Chez Panisse Cooking; James Beard's American Cookery; Leon; New Southern Cooking; The Taste of Country Cooking*

Chimamanda Ngozi Adichie is the author of two novels, including *Half of a Yellow Sun*, which won the Orange Prize in 2007. Her short-story collection *The Thing Around Your Neck* was published in 2009.

The Dark Child; Middlemarch; The Line of Beauty; Arrow of God; Lucy; The Fire Next Time; Reef; Collected Poems [Derek Walcott]; *No Sweetness Here*

Daniel Alarcón is the author of a collection of short stories and the novel *Lost City Radio*, which was published in 2007. He is also a cofounder of Radio Ambulante, a Spanish-language podcast.

Ours; This Way for the Gas, Ladies and Gentlemen; Nowhere Man; Los detectives salvajes [The Savage Detectives]; Flight Without End; Safe Area Gorazde; 2666; The Emperor; La ciudad y los perros [The Time of the Hero]; The Portable Chekhov

Hilton Als is a staff writer for *The New Yorker* and the magazine's theater critic.

Selected Works of Djuna Barnes; Time Regained; The Price of the Ticket; The Dogs Bark; Dancers, Buildings, and People in the Streets; The Portable Hawthorne; Peasants and Other Stories

Paola Antonelli is the senior curator of architecture and design at The Museum of Modern Art in New York.

La via del samurai [The Way of the Samurai]; unidentified high school philosophy textbook; *Project Japan; The Immortal Life of Henrietta Lacks; Architectures expérimentales, 1950–2000; So Far So Goude; Ferrari; The Complete Far Side; Disco Bloodbath; The Independent Group; Underground; The Shock Doctrine; Personal History; White Teeth; Flatlandia; Spoon River Anthology; The Emperor of All Maladies; What Is Your Dangerous Idea?; Cod; Il cucchiaio d'argento [The Silver Spoon]; Hello World; Neuromancer; Fiabe italiane [Italian Folktales]*

Judd Apatow wrote and directed the films *Knocked Up* and *Funny People*. His latest film, *This Is Forty*, will be released in December 2012.

Twenty Thirty; Conversations with Wilder; Adultery and Other Choices; This Boy's Life; Cathedral; If You Want to Write; The Marx Brothers Scrapbook; Monty Python's Big Red Book; Born Standing Up; When Things Fall Apart; The Last Laugh; Flappers and Philosophers; What Is the What; Seize the Day; A Fan's Notes; Ladies and Gentlemen—Lenny

Bruce!!; I'll Sleep When I'm Dead; Do I Have to Give Up Me to Be Loved by You?; A Death in the Family; Among the Missing; Shot in the Heart

Tauba Auerbach is an artist based in New York.

Pac-Mastery; How to Enjoy Reality; Alphabeta Concertina; Ashes to Splashes; Woman with a Camera; Exhaustive Parallel Intervals; Powers of Ten; Down; Local Myths / Love Spells; Catalog for an Exhibition of Book Works; Josh Smith; Cent mille milliards de poémes [A Hundred Million Million Poems]; untitled book; Sigmar Polke: Lens Paintings; Interaction of Color; The Home Planet

Dan Barber is the chef and co-owner of Blue Hill restaurant in New York City, and Blue Hill at Stone Barns in Tarrytown, New York. His first book will be published by The Penguin Press in 2013.

Goodbye, Columbus; Up in the Old Hotel; Song for the Blue Ocean; Cultivating an Ecological Conscience; The Lost Language of Plants; Essential Cuisine [Michel Bras]; Tree Crops; A Sand County Almanac; The Soil and Health; Not for Bread Alone; Nancy Silverton's Breads from the La Brea Bakery; When Nietzsche Wept; The Web of Life; Nature's Operating Instructions; Adventures on the Wine Route; American Pastoral

Jo Ann Beard is the author of *The Boys of My Youth* and *In Zanesville*, which was published by Little, Brown in 2011.

Rabbit Is Rich; Rabbit at Rest; Lives of Girls and Women; My Friend the Dog; The Yearling; Junkyard Dogs and William Shakespeare; The Best American Short Stories, 1995; The End of Vandalism; Matters of Life and Death

Jen Bekman is the owner of her eponymous gallery based in New York City. She is also the founder of 20x200 and Hey, Hot Shot!

The Work of Charles and Ray Eames; Paula Scher; From Here to There: Alec Soth's America; The Penguin Guide to Jazz Recordings; Harriet the Spy; The Elements of Style, Illustrated; Illuminance; Eats, Shoots & Leaves; Ways of Seeing; Family Business; Furthermore; The Experience of Place; Lunch Poems; Then & Now

Coralie Bickford-Smith is a cover designer at Penguin Books.

The History of Danish Dreams; Flappers and Philosophers; Naming Baby; Lettering in Ornament; The War of the Worlds; A Humument; Art Deco Bookbindings; Nineteen Eighty-Four; One of Our Submarines; Dracula; Songs of Innocence & Experience; V&A Pattern: The Fifties; The Unbearable Lightness of Being; Five Hundred Years of Printing

Mark Bittman is a *New York Times* Opinion columnist and the lead food writer for the *New York Times Magazine*. His books include the bestselling *How to Cook Everything* and the groundbreaking *Food Matters*, which explores the crucial connections among food, health, and the environment and provides tangible guidance for Americans rethinking their diets.

Red Harvest; Tom Stoppard: Plays 5; Flow; The Pursuit of Love; Emil Nolde; Yiddishland; Back Where I Came From; The Worst Journey in the World; The Last European War; The Jeeves Omnibus; Living in a World Revolution; The Count of Monte Cristo; Matisse; One Hundred Famous Views of Edo; The Second Sex; New Grub Street; Looking Backward; Catch-22

Sophie Buhai and **Lisa Mayock** are the designers behind the fashion label Vena Cava.

Grapefruit; Hell's Angels; Hard Candy; The Basil and Josephine Stories; The Comedy of Errors; Be Here Now; Man, Myth and Magic, Volume 8; Hollywood Babylon II; The Elegant Universe; 2666; Story of the Eye; The Magus; The Game; The House Book

Rosanne Cash is a singer, songwriter, and author. She has released fourteen albums, including *The List*, which came out in 2009. Her memoir *Composed* was published in 2010.

The War of Art; Le Morte d'Arthur; Love in the Time of Cholera; The Elements of Style; Poems and Plays [Alfred Lord Tennyson]; *Middlemarch; Letters to a Young Poet; The Diary of a Young Girl; On Life After Death; Stanislavsky Directs; How We Die; The Essential Rumi; One Day in the Life of Ivan Denisovich; The Woman's Encyclopedia of Myths and Secrets; Little House in the Big Woods; Here Is New York; Memories, Dreams, Reflections*

Michael Chabon is the author of several short-story collections,

essays, and seven novels, including *The Amazing Adventures of Kavalier & Clay*, which received the Pulitzer Prize for fiction in 2001. His latest novel, *Telegraph Avenue*, was published in 2012.

Swann's Way; Dune; A Wizard of Earthsea; The Fall of the House of Usher and Other Writings; Gravity's Rainbow; Orlando; Labyrinths; The Stories of John Cheever; The Phantom Tollbooth; The Most of S. J. Perelman; The Portable Faulkner; The Long Goodbye; The Adventures of Sherlock Holmes; Cloud Atlas; Blood Meridian; Sixty Stories [Donald Barthelme]; *Airships; At the Mountains of Madness; Love in the Time of Cholera; Ulysses; Moby-Dick*

Candy Chang is an artist, graphic designer, and urban planner. She is a co-founder of Civic Center, a creative studio based in New Orleans that works to make cities more comfortable for people.

Richard Scarry's Best Word Book Ever; New York [Ric Burns]; *City* [William H. Whyte]; *The Little Prince; The Power Broker; The Death and Life of Great American Cities; The Elements of Style, Illustrated; The Image of the City; A Moveable Feast; Life Between Buildings; White Noise; Tibor Kalman, Perverse Optimist; Letters from the Avant-Garde; The Devil in the White City; Archigram; The Orchid Thief; A Little History of the World; Understanding Comics; Essays of E. B. White; Never Let Me Go; Sagmeister; Jimmy Corrigan, The Smartest Kid on Earth*

David Chang is the chef and owner of the Momofuku restaurant group, which includes Momofuku Noodle Bar, Momofuku Ssäm Bar, Momofuku Ko, MáPêche, and Milk Bar in New York City, and Momofuku Seiōbo in Sydney, Australia. David is also the author of the *Momofuku* cookbook and is the co-creator and editor of the quarterly print journal *Lucky Peach*.

La alta cocina vasca en miniatura: pinchos y picas; Préparez terrines, foie gras et sauces a l'école des professionnels; The Big Fat Duck Cookbook; Essential Cuisine [Michel Bras]; *Basic Technology of Soba; Basic Technology of Udon; Applied Technology of Soba/Udon; Coco; El Bulli; Autoritratto della cucina italiana d'avanguardia; The River Cottage Meat Book; La cocina del Restaurante Kursaal Martín Berasategu; El celler de Can Roca: una sinfonía fantástica; The Professional Charcuterie Series: Pates, Terrines and Ballotines Made with Poultry, Veal, Pork and Liver Andouilles and Andouillettes-Foie Gras; Roellinger: trois étoiles de mer; The Forager's Harvest; Bestiarium gastronomicae; Into the Vietnamese Kitchen; Diccionario botanico para cocineros; Mushrooms for Health; Olivier Roellinger's Contemporary French Cuisine; Sergio; Best Ramen of 2003; Soba: A Nationwide Guide to the Best Soba Restaurants; Jean-Georges; Windows on the World Complete Wine Course; Un recorrido por la historia de montagud editores (1906–2006); Quique Dacosta 2000–2006; Mushrooms: Wild and Edible; Bouchon; Roger Vergé's Vegetables in the French Style; Ninja*

Rachel Comey designs her eponymous fashion line, which she launched in 2001.

Varvara Stepanova; Shocking Life; The Native Trees of Canada; The Pathfinders; Toile de Jouy; Sonia Delaunay; Dressed for the Photographer; Trapunto by Machine; Logic & Design; Claire McCardell: Redefining Modernism; Pioneer Women; The Quilts of Gee's Bend; Art Deco and Modernist Carpets; Textiles of the Wiener Werkstätte; Native Funk & Flash; The Pile Weaves; Modernist Jewelry 1930–1960; Seven Arrows; Human Dimension and Interior Space; Soft Jewelry; Hull Pottery; A Second Treasury of Knitting Patterns; Yes; Album [Hannah Höch]; *A World of Head Ornaments*

Robert Crais is the author of the number one *New York Times* best-selling *Elvis Cole* novels. He was the 2006 recipient of the Ross Macdonald Literary Award.

The Glass Teat; Early Autumn; Dangerous Visions; The Martian Chronicles; The Past Through Tomorrow; The Old Man and the Sea; The Little Sister; Stranger in a Strange Land; Tarzan of the Apes; Nine Stories [J. D. Salinger]

Sloane Crosley is the author of two essay collections, including *How Did You Get This Number*, which was published in 2010.

The Writing Life; The Best American Short Stories of the Century; Oh Pure and Radiant Heart; Who Will Run the Frog Hospital?; The Portable Dorothy Parker; Me Talk Pretty One Day; What Is the What; Heartburn; Birds of America; A Supposedly Fun Thing I'll Never Do Again; The Complete Stories [Flannery O'Connor]; *The Great Gatsby; Lolita; Slouching Towards Bethlehem; The Stories of John Cheever; Dubliners*

Adrian Danchig-Waring is a soloist at the New York City Ballet. **Pontus Lidberg** is a choreographer, dancer, and filmmaker based out of Stockholm and New York City.

Siddhartha; Twenty-Eight Artists and Two Saints; The Art of Simple Food; The Art Spirit; The Essential Rumi; Le vieux qui lisait des romans d'amour [The Old Man Who Read Love Stories]; The Essential Duane Michals; The Arrival; Francesca Woodman; Tales from Moominvalley

Tom Delavan is an interior designer based in New York. He is the creative director of GILT Home.

Nine Stories [J. D. Salinger]; *Huis clos [No Exit]; Wuthering Heights; The Tao of Health and Longevity; Cy Twombly; The House Book; The Andy Warhol Diaries; Howard's End; Picturing Ed; Architecture Architektur; Horst Interiors; Living with Design; Le regole dell'attrazione [The Rules of Attraction]; A Clockwork Orange; The Ice Storm; The Sorrows of Young Werther*

Junot Díaz is the author of numerous essays, two short-story collections, and the novel *The Brief Wondrous Life of Oscar Wao*, which won the Pulitzer Prize for fiction in 2008.

The Fellowship of the Ring; The Two Towers; The Return of the King; Planet of the Apes as American Myth; The Woman Warrior; Woman Hollering Creek and Other Stories; Family Installments; Watership Down; A Lexicon of Terror; Dawn; The God of Small Things; The Motion of Light in Water; Miracleman; Love & Rockets No. 12: Poison

River; The Long Night of White Chickens; From Protest to Challenge, Volume 5; Dogeaters; Divided Planet

Simon Doonan is the creative-ambassador-at-large of Barneys New York. He is the author of five books, including *Gay Men Don't Get Fat*, which was published in 2012.

Scruples; A Fairly Honourable Defeat; The Liars' Club; The Idler Book of Crap Towns; The Painted Word; Sex, Art, and American Culture; The Custom of the Country; Spend, Spend, Spend; Sorry I Kept You Waiting, Madam; The Things I Love

Jennifer Egan is a writer and journalist. She is the author of a short-story collection and four novels, including *A Visit from the Goon Squad*, which won the Pulitzer Prize for fiction and the National Book Critics Circle Award for fiction in 2011.

Don Quixote; The Image; Don Juan; The Golden Notebook; Good Morning, Midnight; Emma; Middlemarch; The Life and Opinions of Tristram Shandy, Gentleman; Germinal; Invisible Man; Underworld; The Transit of Venus; The House of Mirth

Dave Eggers is the author of seven books, including *Zeitoun*, which was published in 2009. Eggers is the founder and editor of McSweeney's, an independent publishing house based in San Francisco that produces a quarterly journal, a monthly magazine (*The Believer*), and *Wholphin*, a quarterly DVD of short films and documentaries.

Travel Writing [Peter Ferry]; *Herzog; A Star Called Henry; The*

Known World; Rising Up and Rising Down; Like Life; Lolita; For Whom the Bell Tolls; Nausea; Slouching Towards Bethlehem; The Sheltering Sky; Jesus' Son

Tina Roth Eisenberg is a design blogger, app developer, and entrepreneur.

The Golden Age of Advertising—the 60s; Inspired; Transit; Wisdom; Stimmungsvolles appenzellerland; Typewise; Grid Systems in Graphic Design; Envisioning Information; Josef Müller-Brockmann; The Art of Looking Sideways; Reinventing the Wheel; Serious Drawings; Helvetica; It's Not How Good You Are, It's How Good You Want to Be; Taking Things Seriously; Findet mich das glück? [Will Happiness Find Me?]; ABC3D; Der vierstöckige hausbesitzer; Paul Rand; Der waschküchenschlüssel, oder sas—wenn gott Schweizer ware; Brooklyn [Judith Stonehill]

Merrill Elam and **Mack Scogin** are the two principals of Mack Scogin Merrill Elam Architects, Inc., based in Atlanta, Georgia.

The Next Jerusalem; Caravaggio; Rome of the Renaissance; Francis Bacon; The Projective Cast; Bauhaus 1919–1933; The Quilts of Gee's Bend; A History of Architecture on the Comparative Method; On Beauty and Being Just; As I Lay Dying; Prior Convictions; Picasso: Guernica, Volume 1; John Lautner, Architect; Suh Seok; The Anxiety of Influence; Alice's Adventures in Wonderland; Prehistoric Architecture in the Eastern United States; Rob Mallet-Stevens; Josef Hoffmann; Solomon's Temple; Mariucia; Mr. Jefferson, Architect; The Monkey Grammarian; The Wind-Up Bird Chronicle

Derek Fagerstrom and Lauren Smith are the owners of The Curiosity Shoppe, based in San Francisco. They are also the creative directors of *Pop-Up* magazine and the authors of two books, including *Wallpaper Projects,* which was published in 2009.

The House Book; Suburbia; The Principles of Uncertainty; Guide to Easier Living; Margaret Kilgallen: In the Sweet Bye & Bye; LaPorte, Indiana; Alexander Girard Designs for Herman Miller; Winogrand 1964; The Americans

Drew Gilpin Faust is a historian and the president of Harvard University. She has published six books, including *This Republic of Suffering: Death and the American Civil War,* which was published in 2008.

Just and Unjust Wars; The Sound and the Fury; The Plague; Tinker, Tailor, Soldier, Spy; Absalom, Absalom!; The Interpretation of Cultures; The Uses of the University; The Things They Carried; Dispatches; To Kill a Mockingbird; The Great War and Modern Memory; Poems [Emily Dickinson]; *The Face of Battle; Coming of Age in Mississippi; Le petit prince [The Little Prince]; The Moviegoer; Memoirs and Selected Letters by Ulysses S. Grant; Beloved*

James Franco is a writer, artist, filmmaker and actor.

Macbeth; The Great Gatsby; A Streetcar Named Desire; White Buildings; Golden State; Who's Afraid of Virginia Woolf?; Swann's Way; The Dream Songs; Moby-Dick; The Sound and the Fury; Pale Fire; Blood Meridian; Collected Fictions [Jorge Luis Borges]; *On the Road; Reality*

Hunger; Lolita; Jesus' Son; The Zoo Story; The Turn of the Screw; Tar; Donkey Gospel; Crossing the Water; One Hundred Years of Solitude; Waiting for Godot; Don Quixote; Cannery Row; A Portrait of the Artist as a Young Man; The Short Stories of Ernest Hemingway; As I Lay Dying; House of Leaves; Collected Stories [Raymond Carver]

Sasha Frere-Jones is the pop music critic for *The New Yorker*. He is currently working on a book about how pop signifies, which will be published by Farrar, Straus & Giroux.

Joseph Roth; Pulphead; C'est la Guerre; Species of Spaces and Other Pieces; Spacesuit; I Love Dick; The Film Criticism of Otis Ferguson; On Elegance While Sleeping; Suicide; The Complete Stories [Flannery O' Connor]

Tobias Frere-Jones is a typeface designer. He works with Jonathan Hoefler at Hoefler & Frere-Jones, a New York City type foundry, and he teaches at the Yale University School of Art.

Mathematics; Ounce Dice Trice; Riddley Walker; Specimens of Printing Types Made at Bruce's New York Type Foundry; Leaves of Grass; Miniature Atlas, Borough of Brooklyn; Cosmopolitan World Atlas; The Chairs; Entropy and Art; Contrasts of Form

Ben Fry is a data visualization expert and artist, principal at the design firm Fathom, and co-developer of the computer language Processing. He has published three books, including *Getting Started with Processing* with Casey Reas, which came out in 2010.

Just Curious; Visualizations; Exploratory Data Analysis; Abstracting Craft; On Food and Cooking; Hidden Order; Data Structures and Program Design in C; Apple IIe Technical Reference Manual; Thinking with Type; Labyrinths; The Innocents Abroad, or The New Pilgrims' Progress; On Directing Film; Symbols, Signals, and Noise; Turtles, Termites, and Traffic Jams; Tim Hawkinson; Moneyball; The Isabella Stewart Gardner Museum; Kurt Vonnegut: Slaughterhouse-Five, The Sirens of Titan, Player Piano, Cat's Cradle, Breakfast of Champions, Mother Night; Information Anxiety; The Science Times Book of Genetics

Rivka Galchen is the author of the novel *Atmospheric Disturbances*, which was published in 2008.

John Ashbery: Collected Poems; The Pillow Book of Sei Shōnagon; The Horned Man; The Good Soldier Švejk; Catch-22; Epitaph of a Small Winner; Alice's Adventures in Wonderland and Through the Looking Glass; The Unconsoled; We Have Always Lived in the Castle; Either/ Or; The Third Policeman; The Red and the Black; Philosophical Papers, Volume 1; The Girls of Slender Means; Dearest Father

Atul Gawande practices general and endocrine surgery at Brigham and Women's Hospital in Boston. He is associate professor of surgery at Harvard Medical School and associate professor in the department of health policy and management at the Harvard School of Public Health. A staff writer at *The New Yorker*, he is the author of three books, including *The Checklist Manifesto*, which was published in 2009.

The Lives of a Cell; The Selected Stories of Anton Chekhov; The Man Who Mistook His Wife for a Hat and Other Clinical Tales; A Farewell to Arms; The Complete Sherlock Holmes Collection; The Periodic Table; Facing Unpleasant Facts; The Death of Ivan Ilyich; American Pastoral; The Bullfighter Checks Her Makeup; Invisible Cities; The Year of Magical Thinking; The Right Stuff; The Doctor Stories; What the Dog Saw

Malcolm Gladwell is a staff writer at *The New Yorker* and the author of four books, including *What the Dog Saw,* which was published in 2009.

Texas Tough; On the Rock; Armed Robbers in Action; The Illusion of Free Markets; Popular Crime; The Business of Crime; Ride the Razor's Edge; The Crime Society; Black Mafia; But They All Came Back; The American Mafia; A Family Business

Kim Gordon is an artist and a founding member of Sonic Youth.

Tapping the Source; Mystery Train; The Book; Women in Love; Image of the People; The Lonely Doll; The Diary of Anaïs Nin, Volume 1, 1931–1934; The Diary of Anaïs Nin, Volume 2, 1934–1939; The Diary of Anaïs Nin, Volume 7, 1966–1974; Bad Behavior; Illuminations; Nausea

Philip Gourevitch is a staff writer at *The New Yorker* and the former editor of *The Paris Review.* He is the author of three books, including, most recently, *Standard Operating Procedure: The Ballad of Abu Ghraib,* which was published in 2008.

In a Free State; Les Thibaults [The World of the Thibaults]; Paradise Lost; My Traitor's Heart; The Idiot; Tanakh; McTeague; Moby-Dick; The Plague; Lord Jim; Invisible Man; The Postman Always Rings Twice; The Sibley Guide to Birds; Life Studies and For the Union Dead; Man's Fate; To the Lighthouse; The Americans; A Good Man Is Hard to Find and Other Stories; The Doctor Stories; The Recognitions

Jorie Graham is a poet and the Boylston Professor of Rhetoric and Oratory at Harvard University. She is the author of numerous collections of poetry, including *The Dream of the Unified Field: Selected Poems 1974–1994,* for which she won the Pulitzer Prize in poetry in 1996, and *Place,* which was published in 2012.

The Structure of Verse; Death and Friends; The Complete Poems [Henry Vaughan]; John Keats; Some Trees; When the Rivers Run Dry; Complete Poems [Marianne Moore]; The Collected Poems of Wallace Stevens; The Complete French Poems [Rainer Maria Rilke]; Field Notes from a Catastrophe; Poets of Reality; The Complete Poems [Elizabeth Bishop]; Without an Alphabet, Without a Face; From the First Nine; Selected Poems [William Carlos Williams]; Report from the Besieged City

Andrew Sean Greer is the author of a short-story collection and three novels, including *The Story of a Marriage,* which was published in 2008.

Travels with My Aunt; The Long Goodbye; Maybe; A High Wind in Jamaica; Collected Poems [Wallace Stevens]; Rebecca; Lunch Poems; The Chateau; Chéri; Lolita

Lev Grossman is a senior writer and book critic for *Time* magazine. He is also the author of four novels, including *The Magician King*, which was published in 2011.

The Sword in the Stone; The Magician's Nephew; Ringworld; Collected Fictions [Jorge Luis Borges]; *The Once and Future King; Waiting for Godot; Arcadia; Watchmen; Ulysses; Brideshead Revisited; Gödel, Escher, Bach; Jonathan Strange & Mr. Norrell; Mrs. Dalloway*

Gabrielle Hamilton is the chef and owner of Prune restaurant in New York City. She is also the author of *Blood, Bones, & Butter: The Inadvertent Education of a Reluctant Chef*, which was published in 2011.

The Life of Samuel Johnson; The Summer Before the Dark; To Kill a Mockingbird; Everyone but Thee and Me; Mortal Acts Mortal Words; Pentimento; Bird by Bird; Mrs. Dalloway; Twelfth Night; Just Above My Head; The Holy Bible, King James Version; *Pig Earth; Of Human Bondage; Adventures of Huckleberry Finn; Flavors of the Riviera; The New Making of a Cook*

Daniel Handler is a writer and accordionist. He also writes under the pen name Lemony Snicket. He is the author of three novels as well as the children's novels *A Series of Unfortunate Events*. His most recent book is the teen novel *Why We Broke Up*, with art by Maira Kalman.

The Bears' Famous Invasion of Sicily; The Changeling; Lolita; Angrams; The Black Brook; Fish Preferred; Mrs. Caliban; Moby-Dick; Danny the

Champion of the World; 30: Pieces of a Novel; The Dream Songs; The Complete Poems [Elizabeth Bishop]; *Les fleurs du mal [The Flowers of Evil]; The Long Goodbye; The Wind-Up Bird Chronicle*

Tony Hawk is a professional skateboarder.

All My Friends Are Dead; Permanent Midnight; Fear and Loathing in Las Vegas; America (The Book); Fool the World; I Had Trouble in Getting to Solla Sollew; The Mutt; Saguaro; Holidays in Hell; High Fidelity; Please Kill Me; Endurance; A Child Called "It"; It's Not About the Bike

Todd Hido is a photographer and artist based out of San Francisco. He is the author of eight books including *House Hunting*, which was published in 2001, and *Excerpts from Silver Meadows* in 2012.

All Legs; The Sinful One; Sexology; The Contented Little Pussy Cat; The Ballad of Sexual Dependency; Pictures from Home; Denver; Los Angeles Spring; Park City; Diane Arbus; Between the Two; Edward Hopper

Pico Iyer is an essayist and novelist. He is the author of ten books, including *The Man Within My Head*, which was published in 2012.
The Quiet American; Walden; Mason & Dixon; The Norton Shakespeare; Among the Cities; The Selected Letters of John Keats; Selected Poems [Derek Walcott]; *Zen Mind, Beginner's Mind; Emerson's Essays; Moby-Dick*

Oliver Jeffers is an artist, writer, and illustrator. He is the author of several children's books, including *Stuck,* which was published in 2011.

New Streets and Roads; English for Polish Students; The Downfall; The Homosexual Outlook; The Golden Book Encyclopedia, Books 11 & 12; The Golden Book Encyclopedia, Books 1 & 2; The Golden Book Encyclopedia, Books 3 & 4; Ivanhoe; The Ascent of Everest; Catch-22; The Illustrated Book of Wild Animals of the World; Basic Mathematics; Illustrated Book of Trees

Miranda July is a performance artist, writer, actress, and film-maker. Her most recent film, *The Future,* was released in 2011. Her most recent book, *It Chooses You,* was published in 2011.

The North Star Man; What We Talk About When We Talk About Love; King Kong Theory; Three Novels: The Cloak, The Black Pestilence, The Comb; Ticknor; Peter Fischli & David Weiss; Moholy-Nagy; The Collected Stories of Lydia Davis; Gentlewoman Issue No. 5; Dieter and Dorothy; Sophie Calle: Did You See Me?

Maira Kalman is an illustrator, author, and designer. She is the author of thirteen children's books, including *Max Makes a Million, What Pete Ate,* and *Looking at Lincoln.* She created an illustrated edition of *The Elements of Style* by Strunk and White and also illustrated Michael Pollan's *Food Rules.*

August Sander; The Face of the World; Cecil Beaton's Fair Lady; Speak, Memory; Lolita; A Way of Seeing; The Tanners; Jakob von Gunten;

Man Ray; I Married Adventure; Diane Arbus; Eugène Atget; Water Towers; Maharaja; Ceremonial Uniforms of the World; The Heritage of Dress: Notes on the History and Evolution of Clothes; Writing and Illuminating and Lettering; Bhargava's Standard Illustrated Dictionary

Zachary Kanin is a staff writer for *Saturday Night Live* and a cartoonist for *The New Yorker.* He is the author of *The Short Book.*

Black Hole; Tales Designed to Thrizzle; The Portable Frank; A Good Man Is Hard to Find and Other Stories; The Wind-Up Bird Chronicle; Midnight's Children; Dangerous Laughter; Jesus' Son; The Princess Bride; Rabbit, Run; Criminal; Cloud Atlas; Birds of America; Middlesex; Tooth and Claw; A Confederacy of Dunces; The Lagoon; Where I'm Calling From; Like a Velvet Glove Cast in Iron; Omega; A.L.I.E.E.E.N.; CivilWarLand in Bad Decline

Mary Karr has published four books of poetry and three memoirs, including *Lit: A Memoir,* which was published in 2009.

One Hundred Years of Solitude; The House at Pooh Corner; Anna Karenina; Speak, Memory; Stories of Anton Chekhov; Selected Poems of Ezra Pound; Dispatches; John Keats; The Palm at the End of the Mind; Nine Stories [J. D. Salinger]; *The Seven Storey Mountain; Selected Poems* [T.S. Eliot]; *Blood Meridian; The Riverside Shakespeare; Geography III; The Once and Future King; High Windows; To Kill a Mockingbird; The Woman Warrior*

Thomas Keller is a chef and restaurateur, most notably of Per Se and The French Laundry, which have both been awarded three Michelin stars. He was granted the insignia of Chevalier of the French Legion of Honor for his promotion of French cuisine in America. He is also the author of four cookbooks, including the *New York Times* bestseller *Ad Hoc at Home*. His *Bouchon Bakery Cookbook* will be released in November 2012.

Le répertoire de la cuisine; Smashed Potatoes; Hering's Dictionary of Classical and Modern Cookery; La Technique; The Standing and the Waiting; Wooden; The 33 Strategies of War; Ma Cuisine; Kiyomi Mikuni; Jean-Louis; Great Chefs of France; Paul Bocuse's French Cooking; Neil Leifer; Freedom; Mastering the Art of French Cooking; On Food and Cooking; La cuisine c'est beaucoup plus que des recettes; The New Larousse Gastronomique; Blue Trout and Black Truffles; An Exaltation of Larks; Just Enough Liebling; The Impossible Takes Longer; Ma Gastronomie; A Treasury of Great Recipes; Plain Speaking

David Kelley is the founder and chairman of the renowned design and innovation consultancy IDEO. He is founder of the Hasso Plattner Institute of Design at Stanford University, where he also is the Donald W. Whittier professor in Mechanical Engineering.

The Work of Ettore Sottsass and Associates; Experiences in Visual Thinking; Copies in Seconds; The Care and Feeding of Ideas; The Art of Innovation; The Ten Faces of Innovation; Self-Efficacy; An Incomplete Education; Thus Spake David E.; The Little Prince; Porsche by Mailander; Ferrari by Mailander

Chuck Klosterman is a consulting editor at Grantland.com. He is the author of several essay collections, nonfiction books, and two novels, including *The Visible Man*, which was published in 2011.

Loose Balls; The Devil & Sherlock Holmes; All My Friends Are Going to Be Strangers; The Ecstasy of Influence; Bitter Harvest; Four Arguments for the Elimination of Television; Where I'm Calling From; The Man Who Loved Only Numbers; A Supposedly Fun Thing I'll Never Do Again; A Season on the Brink; The Fourth Dimension; The Fifties; The Warren Commission Report; Spin Alternative Record Guide

Lawrence Lessig is the director of the Edmond J. Safra Foundation Center for Ethics at Harvard University and a professor of law at Harvard Law School. He is the author six books, including *Republic, Lost: How Money Corrupts Congress—and a Plan to Stop It*, which was published in 2011.

The Common Law; Snow Crash; Philosophy and the Mirror of Nature; The Fountainhead; Philosophical Investigations; Ten Days That Shook the World; The Logic of Collective Action; Moral Scepticism and Moral Knowledge; Three Novels of Ernest Hemingway; Notes of Debates in the Federal Convention of 1787; Copyright in Historical Perspective; To the Lighthouse; Language & Symbolic Power; False Necessity; We the People, Volume 1; The Subjection of Women; The Federalist Papers; Anarchy, State, and Utopia; A Theory of Justice; The Custom of the Country; Toward a Feminist Theory of the State; The Decision to Use the Atomic Bomb and the Architecture of an American Myth; Metaphysics and the Philosophy of Mind; Howards End

Jonathan Lethem is the author of several books, essay collections, and novels, including *Chronic City*, which was published in 2009.

The Thurber Carnival; Crazy in Berlin; Everything You Need; If on a Winter's Night a Traveler; A Mother's Kisses; The Land of Laughs; Sleepless Nights; The Shipwrecked; Hopscotch; Walking Small; The Deadly Percheron; A Servant's Tale; The Best of William Irish; Beautiful Losers

Yiyun Li is the author of two short-story collections and the novel *The Vagrants*, which was published in 2009.

The House in Paris; Monsignor Quixote; The Collected Stories [William Trevor]; A Moveable Feast; Before My Time; Turgenev's Letters; Essays of Michel de Montaigne; The Living Novel and Later Appreciations; Willie ille pu [Winnie the Pooh]; One Art

Pamela Love is the designer and founder of her eponymous jewelry line, which was started in 2006.

Francesco Clemente; Hollywood Babylon; Tropic of Capricorn; 7000 Years of Jewelry; Art Forms in Nature; Cabinet of Natural Curiosities; The Complete Costume History; Lee Bontecou; Georgia O'Keeffe and the Camera; Shakey; Magick in Theory and Practice; North American Indian Jewelry and Adornment; Psychomagic; Bury My Heart at Wounded Knee; Utopia Parkway; Cathedral; Our Band Could Be Your Life; Slouching Towards Bethlehem; Jesus' Son; The Catcher in the Rye

Larissa MacFarquhar is a staff writer for *The New Yorker*. She is currently writing a book about extremely ethical lives, which will be published by The Penguin Press.

What Maisie Knew; Everything That Rises Must Converge; Art and Objecthood; Life & Times of Michael K; Studies on Hysteria; Collected Poems [Philip Larkin]; Culture and Value; The Good Soldier; Profiles; T. S. Eliot: Collected Poems, 1909–1962; Against Theory; Madness and Civilization; In Dreams Begin Responsibilities and Other Stories; Fathers and Sons; Mortal Questions

John Maeda is a graphic designer, computer scientist, and president of the Rhode Island School of Design. He is the author of nine books, including *Redesigning Leadership*, which was published in 2011.

Artful Sentences; A Picture Storybook; The C Programming Language; Good to Great; How to Do Things with Videogames; The Forms of Color; Biology Coloring Workbook; Paul Rand; Self-Renewal; Grid Systems in Graphic Design; ZONE 1/2; It's Not About the Coffee; Better; A Brief History of Curating; Norm & Form; Flatland

Stephin Merritt is a singer and songwriter. He belongs to four bands: the Magnetic Fields, the 6ths, the Gothic Archies, and Future Bible Heroes.

The Oxford English Dictionary, Volume XX; The King's Stilts; Look, I Made a Hat; The Folk Songs of North America in the English Language; Polka Happiness; The League of Extraordinary Gentlemen, Volume III;

Clockwork Music; Crowds and Power; Manners from Heaven; Novellas and Other Writings [Edith Wharton]; *The Golden Gate; Berlin Alexanderplatz; The Young Visiters or, Mr. Salteena's Plan; The Complete Rhyming Dictionary and Poet's Craft Book; London Mini Street Atlas*

Stephenie Meyer is the author of the number one bestselling Twilight Saga and *The Host*.

Neverwhere; Pride and Prejudice; Rebecca; The Book of a Thousand Days; Anne of Green Gables; Jane Eyre; The Princess Bride; Little Women; The Book of Mormon; *Dragonflight; East of Eden; Ararat; Speaker for the Dead*

Marilyn Minter is an artist based in New York City.

Diane Arbus; de Kooning; Bellefleur; Andersen's Fairy Tales; Been There, Done That; The Philosophy of Andy Warhol; The Andy Warhol Diaries; A Visit from the Goon Squad; Lee Miller; A Little Original Sin; Pleasure and Danger; Atonement; Matisse the Master

Thurston Moore is a songwriter and musician. He is a founding member of the band Sonic Youth.

Where I Hang My Hat; Wishes, Lies, and Dreams; Satori in Paris; Chic Death; The Aesthetics of Rock; A Bibliography of Works by Allen Ginsberg; The Cosmological Eye; Seventh Heaven

Nico Muhly a classical music composer. He has worked on numerous films, orchestral works, operas, ensembles, and other mu-

sical projects. He has also released seven albums, including *Seeing Is Believing*, from 2011.

A Stolen Life; The Hindus; Unspeakable; Vietnamese Street Food; The Swimming-Pool Library; Mitzvah Girls; Jerusalem; Kim Jong-Il; the Wycliffe New Testament; *Rose West; Any Human Heart; Caligula for President*

Kate and **Laura Mulleavy** are the fashion designers behind the label Rodarte, which was created in 2005.

Great Expectations; Spring Snow; Songs of Innocence & of Experience; The Catcher in the Rye; Pale Fire; The Destructors; Ulysses; To Kill a Mockingbird; John Muir in Yosemite; Sons and Lovers; The Outsiders; Frankenstein; The Raven; The Grapes of Wrath; The Call of the Wild; Notes from Underground; A Confederate General from Big Sur; On the Road; The Mysteries of Udolpho; Blood Meridian; Tess of the d'Urbervilles; Absalom, Absalom!; The Silence of the Lambs

Mira Nair is a filmmaker and producer. She has directed twenty-two films, including *The Reluctant Fundamentalist*, which will be released in 2013.

Light on Yoga; Collected Poems of Dylan Thomas 1934–1952; A Suitable Boy; The Peacock's Egg; The Namesake; The Reluctant Fundamentalist; Guru Dutt; Geoffrey Bawa; Henri Cartier-Bresson; Sea of Poppies; Swami on Rye; Good Muslim, Bad Muslim; Midnight's Children; Things I Didn't Know I Loved; One Hundred Years of Solitude; River of Colour; Evening Ragas; Henri Cartier-Bresson in India; The Americans; The

Democratic Forest; Parsis; Poems by Faiz; The Life and Works of Sadat Hassan Manto; Shah of Shahs; I Write What I Like; From Citizen to Refugee; Privacy

Christoph Niemann is an illustrator and the author of several illustrated books, including *Abstract City,* which was published in 2012.

Raymond Pettibon; A Supposedly Fun Thing I'll Never Do Again; Hitch 22; Dürer—Cranach—Holbein; Der meister und margarita [The Master and Margarita]; Anatomie für künstler [Anatomy for the Artist]; Personal History; Freedom; Out of Sheer Rage; On Writing; Facing Unpleasant Facts; Ich habe den englischen könig bedient [I Served the King of England]; The Dalkey Archive; Irischer lebenslauf

Sigrid Nunez is the author of six novels, including *Salvation City,* which was published in 2010. She is also the author of *Sempre Susan: A Memoir of Susan Sontag,* published in 2011.

Dispatches; Four in Hand; Household Tales by Brothers Grimm; I Remember; The Berlin Stories; A Woman in Berlin; Mythology [Edith Hamilton]; *Journey Around My Room; Boyhood; The Collected Stories of Lydia Davis; My Dog Tulip; Black Lamb and Grey Falcon; The Notebooks of Malte Laurids Brigge; The Collected Prose* [Elizabeth Bishop]; *The Complete Poems, 1927–1979* [Elizabeth Bishop]; *Dreams of a Robot Dancing Bee; The Oxford Book of Death; The Meadow*

James Patterson is a bestselling novelist known for his thrill-ers, including the Alex Cross, Michael Bennett, and Women's Murder Club series, as well as his bestselling books for kids, including *Maximum Ride, Witch & Wizard,* and *Middle School, The Worst Years of My Life.*

The Friends of Eddie Coyle; Red Dragon; California Fire and Life; Ninety-Two in the Shade; Nine Horses; The Path to Power; One Hundred Years of Solitude; Mrs. Bridge; Mr. Bridge; Different Seasons; The Book Thief; The Bed of Procrustes; The Forever War; Lush Life; Matterhorn; Fear and Loathing in Las Vegas; How to Live

Nancy Pearl is a librarian and the author of several books, including the Book Lust series. *Book Lust to Go: Recommended Reading for Travelers, Vagabonds, and Dreamers* was published in 2010.

The Underpainter; A Step Beyond Innocence; The Soul of Viktor Tronko; Souls Raised from the Dead; The Easy Way Out; A Gay and Melancholy Sound; The Lion in the Lei Shop; Cryptonomicon; One Sweet Quarrel; Plum & Jaggers; At War as Children; Things Invisible to See

Francine Prose is the author of more then twenty books of fiction and nonfiction, including *Reading Like a Writer* and, most recently, a novel, *My New American Life,* which was published in 2011.

The Kiss and Other Stories; Selected Stories [Anton Chekhov]; *Notebook of Anton Chekhov; The Duel; The Witch; The Lady with the Dog; The Horse-Stealers; Love; The Selected Letters of Anton Chekhov;*

Ward Six and Other Stories; Stories [Anton Chekhov]; *Last Stories* [Anton Chekhov]; painted wooden book of *Love and Other Stories* [Anton Chekhov] by Leanne Shapton

Ishmael Reed is a poet, novelist, essayist, songwriter, playwright, cartoonist, and jazz musician. He has published six poetry collections and ten novels, including *Juice!*, from 2011. He taught for thirty-five years at the University of California. He is a Harvard Signet Fellow and a Yale Calhoun Fellow.

Freedmen, Philanthropy, and Fraud; Rediscovering America; Yearning; The Complete Works of Nathanael West; The Nazi Connection; Showing Out; Black Girl from Tannery Flats; White Lies; Racial Matters; Under the Blankettes; City Beautiful; Maud Martha; Black Warriors; The Man Who Cried I Am; Black Boy; Yellow Black; Julius Streicher; Street Justice; Warriors, Conjurers and Priests; The Negro Church in America / The Black Church Since Frazier

Alex Ross is the music critic for *The New Yorker*. He is the author of *The Rest Is Noise* and *Listen to This*.

Mythologies; The Tempest; The Palm at the End of the Mind; The Infinite Variety of Music; Ulysses; The Collected Poems of W.B. Yeats; Blue Nights; The Varieties of Religious Experience; Doctor Faustus; The Proud Tower; Silence; The Rings of Saturn; Symphony No. 9 [Mahler]; *The American*

Stefan Sagmeister is a graphic designer and typographer. He is

the owner of Sagmeister Inc., based in New York City, and the author of *Sagmeister: Made You Look*, with Peter Hall, as well as *Things I Have Learned in My Life So Far*, which was published in 2008.

Sugimoto; Hiroshi Sugimoto; Passage; Manufactured Landscapes; Ente, tod und tulpe [Duck, Death and the Tulip]; Hong Kong / China Photographers Two; Sol Lewitt; Adolf Wölfli; A Supposedly Fun Thing I'll Never Do Again; The Corrections; The Happiness Hypothesis; What I Loved

George Saunders is the author of five books of fiction and *The Braindead Megaphone*, a collection of essays, which was published in 2007.

Life and Fate; Red Cavalry and Other Stories; The Portable Chekhov; Dead Souls; The Collected Stories [Nikolai Gogol]; *The Bluest Eye; Moby-Dick; Hadji Murad; Tristram Shandy; Doctor Zhivago; A Confederacy of Dunces; Madame Bovary; White Teeth; Infinite Jest; Today I Wrote Nothing; On the Road; Back in the World; The Coast of Chicago; Cannery Row; The Collected Stories of Lydia Davis*

Ben Schott is a writer, photographer, and author of the *Schott's Miscellanies* and *Schott's Almanac* series.

The Doubtful Guest; The Gulag Archipelago; Forty Years On and Other Plays; The Human Factor; Abram Games, Graphic Designer; Ishihara's Tests for Colour-Blindness; Under Milk Wood; John Heartfield; Decline and Fall; The London Encyclopaedia; The Compact Oxford English

Dictionary; Very Good, Jeeves; The Wind-Up Bird Chronicle; Othello [Braille edition]; *Discipline and Punish; Arcadia; The Intellectuals and the Masses; The Life of Samuel Johnson*

David Sedaris is the author of eight books including *Naked, Me Talk Pretty One Day,* and *Squirrel Seeks Chipmunk: A Modest Bestiary,* which was published in 2010.

The Easter Parade; Jenny & the Jaws of Life; Them; Everything Ravaged, Everything Burned; Cathedral; Birds of America; Random Family; The Barracks Thief; Revolutionary Road; Among the Thugs; The Complete Stories [Flannery O'Connor]; *The Portable Dorothy Parker; Metropolitan Life; The Night in Question; An Obedient Father; In the Garden of the North American Martyrs*

Leanne Shapton is a writer, artist, and illustrator. She is the author of four books, including *Swimming Studies,* which was published in June 2012.

End Zone; The Loser; Pierre Le-Tan; Rebecca; Cakes; Cox Codex 1; Vernacular Drawings; Thomas Struth: Strangers and Friends; David Hockney Photographs; Revealing Illustrations; End of an Age; Haunts of the Black Masseur; Alle kleider einer frau [All the Clothes of a Woman]; A Severed Head; The Kitchen Diaries; Restless Spirits; The Boys of My Youth; Lady into Fox; Women of Paris

Sally Singer is the editor of the *New York Times T Magazine.* Prior to that, she was the fashion news and features director at *Vogue.*

Shuffle; The Hidden Injuries of Class; Collected Poems [Thom Gunn]; *Even Cowgirls Get the Blues; In the Western Night; Dancing Girls; The Emperor; London Fields; The Collected Stories* [Grace Paley]; *Everything That Rises Must Converge; Love in a Cold Climate; The Sound and the Fury; Look at Me; Invisible Man; The Adversary; Break It Down; Snow; In Dreams Begin Responsibilities and Other Stories; Waterland; The Conquest of America*

Nadia Sirota is a violist based in New York City. Her album *First Things First* was released in 2009.

Martha Stewart: Just Desserts; Harry Potter and the Order of the Phoenix; The Rest Is Noise; The Listening Composer; The Amazing Adventures of Kavalier & Clay; Holidays on Ice; Colors Insulting to Nature; Cruddy; Infinite Jest; Blood, Bones & Butter; The Golden Compass; Our Band Could Be Your Life; A Clockwork Orange; Jimmy Corrigan: The Smartest Kid on Earth

Aria Beth Sloss is the author of the debut novel *Autobiography of Us,* which will be published in February 2013 by Henry Holt.

American Primitive; Jane Eyre; Memory Wall; Silent Spring; Mrs. Dalloway; The Changing Light at Sandover; Pilgrim at Tinker Creek; Ulysses; The Gardens of Kyoto; Dancing After Hours; Lolita; The Last Samurai; The Metamorphoses of Ovid; The Story of a Marriage; Housekeeping; The Cocktail Party

Patti Smith is a singer-songwriter, poet, and visual artist. She has released ten albums. Her memoir *Just Kids* was published in 2010 and won the National Book Award for nonfiction.

A Season in Hell [two copies]; *My Life in the Bush of Ghosts; Rasa; The Man Without Qualities, Volume 1; Collected Poems, 1947–1980* [Allen Ginsberg]; *In Country Sleep; Queer; Letters to His Family and Friends, Volume 1; Ariel; Les fleurs du mal [The Flowers of Evil]*

Alec Soth is a photographer based in Minneapolis, Minnesota. He has published six books of photography, including *Sleeping by the Mississippi*, from 2006. He is the founder of Little Brown Mushroom Books.

Hareta Hi / A Fine Day; Pictures from Home; Treadwell; The Palm at the End of the Mind; A Shimmer of Possibility, Volumes 1–12; Love on the Left Bank; Suite Vénitienne / Please Follow Me; Winterreise; Lucian Freud Paintings; Stephen Shore; Looking for Love; How to Hide Anything; William Eggleston's Guide; U-NI-TY; Selected Poems [William Carlos Williams]; *Winesburg, Ohio; The Mezzanine; Beauty in Photography; Jesus' Son; Edith & Big Bad Bill; The Solitude of Ravens; Social Graces: Photographs by Larry Fink; Summer Nights; Alice Neel*

Scott Spencer has written ten novels, including *Man in the Woods*, which was published in 2010.

Enemies, A Love Story; Howl and Other Poems; Evergreen Review, Volume 5, Number 16; Revolutionary Road; The Complete Short Sto-ries of Ernest Hemingway; Letting Go; The Stories of John Cheever; A Mother's Kisses; Beyond the Bedroom Wall; Pale Fire; The Golden Notebook; A Burnt-Out Case

Lorin Stein is the editor of *The Paris Review*. Prior to that, he worked as an editor at Farrar, Straus & Giroux.

The End of the Novel of Love; Studies in Classic American Literature; The Arabian Nights; The Complete Works and Letters of Charles Lamb; Chuck Amuck; William Shakespeare: Comedies, Volumes 1 and 2; William Shakespeare: Histories; William Shakespeare: Tragedies/ Poems; The Oxford Anthology of English Literature Volume I; The Oxford Anthology of English Literature Volume II; The Penguin Book of French Poetry; Infinite Jest; Must We Mean What We Say?; Loving; English Costume from the 14th through the 19th Century; The Poetical Works of Keats; The Education of Henry Adams; To the Lighthouse; Les fleurs du mal [The Flowers of Evil]; Life on the Mississippi; Pulphead; Swann's Way

John Jeremiah Sullivan is a contributing writer to the *New York Times Magazine*, a contributing editor to *Harper's* magazine, and the southern editor of *The Paris Review*. He has written two books, including *Pulphead*, which was published in 2011.

Doctor Zhivago; King Henry IV, Parts 1 and 2; 7 Greeks; The Diary of Samuel Pepys, Volume 1; The Diary of Samuel Pepys, Volume 2; The Ethics, Treatise on the Emendation of the Intellect, and Selected Letters; Old New York: False Dawn; Old New York: The Old Maid; Old

New York: The Spark; Old New York: New Year's Day; Swiss Family Robinson; The Waste Books; The Life of Samuel Johnson; A blank leather-bound journal

Christina Tosi is the chef and owner of Momofuku Milk Bar. She is also the author of the *Momofuku Milk Bar* cookbook, which was published in 2011.

Molecular Gastronomy; A Confederacy of Dunces; Atlas Shrugged; The Joy of Cooking; Sick Puppy; Childcraft: The How and Why Library, Volume 7: How Things Work; Childcraft: The How and Why Library, Volume 11: Make and Do; Kitchen Confidential; Russian Criminal Tattoo Encyclopaedia, Volume I; The Sirens of Titan; The Member of the Wedding; Reader's Digest Complete Do-It-Yourself Manual; The Last American Man; The New York Times Cookbook; The Bell Jar; Still Life with Woodpecker; El Bulli; On Food and Cooking

Wells Tower is a writer and journalist. He is the author of *Everything Ravaged, Everything Burned,* which was published in 2009.

The Book of Ebenezer Le Page; Geronimo Rex; The Collected Stories of Richard Yates; Family; The Complete Stories [Flannery O'Connor]; *Essays of E.B. White; The Moviegoer; Mrs. Bridge; Independent People; Four Quartets; An Age Like This; My Country Right or Left; As I Please; In Front of Your Nose; Gringos; Palm-of-the-Hand Stories; The 13 Clocks*

Gina Trapani is an app developer and blogger. She created the

social media analytics software ThinkUp, and she is the founding editor of the blog Lifehacker.

Leaves of Grass; Getting Things Done; Light a Single Candle; On Writing; The God Delusion; The War of Art; The Clan of the Cave Bear; Rubyfruit Jungle; The Dream of a Common Language; Lunch Poems; Tipping the Velvet; A Wrinkle in Time; Bird by Bird; Harriet the Spy; Moby-Dick; A Whole New Mind; The Lion, the Witch and the Wardrobe; Fight Club; Night

Jakob Trollbäck is a designer. He is the co-founder and creative director of Trollbäck + Company, based in New York City.

Visionaire 40: Roses; Josef Müller-Brockman; Thomas Struth; The Book of Shrigley; The Red Book; Gerhard Richter: Atlas; Le Corbusier Le Grand; Araki by Araki; Shigeru Ban; Richard Prince; Dispatches from the Tenth Circle; Ludwig Wittgenstein; The Annotated Alice; The Kindness of Women; South of the Border, West of the Sun; Shantaram; The Book of 101 Books; Designing Design; Once

Robert Verdi is a stylist and fashion television host. He currently stars on *The Robert Verdi Show* on Logo.

The Hermès Scarf; The Cultivated Life; Yves Saint Laurent; The Stephen Sprouse Book; Legendary Parties, 1922–1972; Tim Walker Pictures; Pierre Cardin; Backstage Dior; Chanel; Elsa Schiaparelli; Diane; Natural Fashion; Emilio Pucci; Louis Vuitton; Rare Bird of Fashion; Simply Halston; The Beautiful Fall; Andy Warhol: Making Money

Vendela Vida is a founding editor of *The Believer* and the author of three novels, including *The Lovers,* which was published in 2010.

The Comfort of Strangers; A Heart So White; The Unbearable Lightness of Being; The Group; After Henry; The Lover; Crime and Punishment; Disgrace; Sleepless Nights; Getting Married; The Razor's Edge; Inferno; Clarissa

Ayelet Waldman is the author of an essay collection and several novels, including *Red Hook Road,* which was published in 2010.
Old Filth; The Queen's Gambit; We Have Always Lived in the Castle; The Innocent; The Amazing Adventures of Kavalier & Clay; A House for Mr. Biswas; Bleak House; Midnight's Children; What Is the What; The English Patient; Persuasion; Mother's Milk

Alice Waters is a restaurateur, author, activist, and proprietor of Chez Panisse Restaurant and Café in Berkeley, California. She is the creator of The Edible Schoolyard and is the vice president of Slow Food International. She is the author of ten books, including *The Art of Simple Food,* which was published in 2007. Her most recent book, *40 Years of Chez Panisse: The Power of Gathering,* came out in 2011.

The French Menu Cookbook; Elizabeth David Classics; The Kindness of Strangers; Contemporary Artists: Olafur Eliasson; Sacred Food; Pomp and Sustenance; A Platter of Figs and Other Recipes; The Taste of Country Cooking; The Cuisines of Mexico; My Bombay Kitchen; Consider the

Oyster; The Auberge of the Flowering Hearth; Adventures on the Wine Route; Nature Morte; A Pattern Language; Second Nature; The Man Who Planted Trees; And the Pursuit of Happiness; Memories of Childhood [Marcel Pagnol]; *Ordinary Resurrections; Fast Food Nation; Slow Food Nation; New Roots for Agriculture; What Are People For?; The One-Straw Revolution; The Value of Nothing; The Magic of Fire; The Secret of Childhood*

William Wegman is a video artist, conceptualist, photographer, painter, and writer based in New York City.

The Golden Book Encyclopedia, Volume 2; Richard Halliburton's Book of Marvels; Childcraft, Volume 3; Betty Crocker's New Picture Cookbook; The World Book Encyclopedia, Volume 8; Science for All; Tell Me Why; The First Book of Surprising Facts; Girl Scout Badges and Signs; Nature Crafts; Your Wonderful World of Science; A Golden Picture Book of Nature Walks; The Hardy Boys: The House on the Cliff; The Hardy Boys: The Secret of the Old Mill; Explorer Manual; Handbook for Boys

George Weld is a cook, farmer, writer, and restaurateur. He founded Egg restaurant and Parish Hall restaurant in New York City and Goatfell Farm in upstate New York.

Holy Bible [Concordance Dictionary: New International Version]; *The Book of Common Prayer; Diet for a Small Planet; Encyclopedia Brown Saves the Day; The Hardy Boys Detective Handbook; Essentials of Classic Italian Cooking; All the King's Men; Desert Solitaire;*

Never Cry Wolf; Sex, Economy, Freedom & Community; The Collected Poems of Wallace Stevens; The Complete Poems and Plays [T. S. Eliot]; *Tao Teh Ching; The Portable Nietzsche; Suttree*

Megan Whitmarsh is a fine artist living and working in Los Angeles.

Selected Poems of Emily Dickinson; The Woman in the Dunes; Petit-Bleu et Petit-Jaune; Death in Midsummer and Other Stories; VALIS; Memoirs of a Shy Pornographer; The Passion According to G.H.; Nine Stories [J. D. Salinger]; *Jane Eyre; Kristin Lavransdatter; Living on the Earth; Meditating with Children; Traces; Cybernetic Serendipity; Les aventures de Tintin: les sept boules de cristal [The Adventures of Tintin: The Seven Crystal Balls]; Rock Dreams; Native Funk & Flash; Powr Mastrs, Volume 1; The Prophet; James M. Cain: Three Complete Novels*

Henry Sene Yee is a cover designer, photographer, and creative director of Picador.

William Eggleston's Guide; Los Alamos; Paul Rand; The Modern Poster; The Graphic Language of Neville Brody; This Is New York; How to Cook Everything; The Vampire Lestat; Classic Book Jackets;

Batman HUSH; Crushed; The Americans; The Amazing Adventures of Kavalier & Clay; Middlesex; The Secret History; The Wind-Up Bird Chronicle; The New York Trilogy; Lolita; Breakfast of Champions; The Great Gatsby; It's Not How Good You Are, It's How Good You Want to Be; The Sun Also Rises; The Catcher in the Rye

Jonathan Zittrain is a professor of law at Harvard Law School and the Harvard Kennedy School, a professor of computer science at the Harvard School of Engineering and Applied Sciences, and a co-founder of Harvard's Berkman Center for Internet & Society. He is the author of *The Future of the Internet—And How to Stop It*, and serves on the boards of the Internet Society and the Electronic Frontier Foundation.

The Elegant Universe; Macbeth; Technopoly; The Complete Maus; Mythology [Edith Hamilton]; *The Foundation Trilogy; The Phantom Tollbooth; The Mind's I; Hyperion; Now We Are Six; A Game of Thrones; The Sandman, Volume 1: Preludes & Nocturnes; Code; Internetworking with TCP/IP, Volume 1; Catch-22; The Rise and Fall of the Third Reich; A Prayer for Owen Meany; The Canon of American Legal Thought; The Age of Missing Information; Cryptonomicon*

Acknowledgments

This book would not have been possible without the hard work of our agents, Kate Lee and Jennifer Joel, and the guidance of our editor, Michael Sand. Thank you for this incredible opportunity.

We are forever indebted to our friends and colleagues who opened up their address books to us. Without you we would have had an entirely different (and far less interesting) book: Dibs Baer, Alexander Benenson, Ami Boghani, Dan Bomze, Kathleen Bomze, Jessica Bremner, Connie Brothers, Sarah Chalfant, Georgia Cool, Lauren Cornell, Sara Distin, Deirdre Foley-Mendelssohn, Macy Halford, Elizabeth Hurchalla, John Knight, Stephanie LaCava, Eric Lach, Jason Ojalvo, Dan Parham, Bre Pettis, Rachel Pike, Caitlin Roper, Emma Straub, Katherine Stirling, Alexis Swerdloff, David Wallace-Wells, and Jenna Wortham.

Much gratitude is owed to those who gave either their time or their counsel: Thomas Gebremedhin, Natalie Jacoby, Maira Kalman, Sara Martin, Shannon McGarity, Dina Nayeri, Anna Noyes, Jason Polan, Devika Rege, Nicole Rudick, Lorin Stein, Anthony Vanger, and Elizabeth Weiss. And a special thanks to Jen Bekman and Andrea Walker in particular, who were both early shepherds of *My Ideal Bookshelf*.

To all of the early fans of this project and our contributors (as well as their assistants and managers), thank you for letting us paint your books. And thank you for sharing your favorite books and your passion for reading with the world.

To bookstores large and small, thank you for letting us photograph the spines of your books for this project. Reading is discovery, and we hope that places like the Strand and Prairie Lights will always be around.

And finally, we would like to thank our families and loved ones: Darko Karas, Zvonko Karas, Charmaine Ehrhart, Kepler Ehrhart Mount, Phoenix Ehrhart Mount, Madison Mount, Sharon Mount, and the Schweizer-Frei family. As well as Fred Benenson, Annaliese La Force, Norman La Force, Ming-Li Wang, and Donna Benenson. Your patience, generosity, enthusiasm, and encouragement go beyond what we could have ever asked for.

About the Authors

Jane Mount is an artist and illustrator who was born in Atlanta and formed in Manhattan. In past incarnations, she has studied anthropology, cofounded three companies, and won awards for her graphic and interior design skills. She is now living in the woods of northern California with her Swiss husband and two cats. Her ideal bookshelf would include Norton Juster's *The Phantom Tollbooth,* Maira Kalman's *The Principles of Uncertainty,* Neil Gaiman's *American Gods, One Hundred Years of Solitude* by Gabriel García Márquez, Jason Polan's *The Every Piece of Art in the Museum of Modern Art Book, The Diamond Age* by Neal Stephenson, *A Suitable Boy* by Vikram Seth, Tracy Kidder's *The Soul of a New Machine,* David Mitchell's *Cloud Atlas,* and books of art by David Hockney, Howard Finster, Fischli & Weiss, and Alice Neel.

Thessaly La Force divides her time between New York City and Iowa City, where she attends the Iowa Writers' Workshop. Prior to that, she worked at the *Paris Review, The New Yorker,* and the New York Public Library. Her ideal bookshelf would include Zadie Smith's *White Teeth,* Jennifer Egan's *A Visit from the Goon Squad,* Joan Didion's *Slouching towards Bethlehem,* Isak Dinesen's *Out of Africa,* Roberto Bolaño's *Savage Detectives,* and Leanne Shapton's *Was She Pretty?* Like Jane, she has two cats; the two women also share the same birthday.